Mark Twain

and the

Jumping Frog of Calaveras County

*How Mark Twain's humorous frog story
launched his legendary writing career.*

George J. Williams III

Tree By The River Publishing
Web site:Autographed-Books.com
e mail address: gjw@aol.com
P.O. Box 20703-CC
Carson City, Nevada 89721 USA

Published by:
Tree By The River Publishing   www.autographed-books.com
P.O. Box 20703-NE
Carson City, Nevada 89721
e mail: gjw@aol.com

Non-fiction books by George Williams III:

Rosa May: The Search For A Mining Camp Legend (1979)
The Guide to Bodie and Eastern Sierra Historic Sites (1982)
The Redlight Ladies of Virginia City, Nevada (1984)
The Murders at Convict Lake (1984)
The Songwriter's Demo Manual and Success Guide (1984 revised 1999)
Mark Twain: His Life In Virginia City, Nevada (1986)
Mark Twain: His Adventures at Aurora and Mono Lake (1987)
Mark Twain and the Jumping Frog of Calaveras County (1999)
Hot Springs of the Eastern Sierra (1988 revised 1996)
Hot Springs of Nevada (1996)
Hot Springs of Northern California (1998)
On the Road with Mark Twain in California and Nevada (1995)
In the Last of the Wild West (1992, revised 1994 and 1999)

Library of Congress Cataloging-in-Publication Data

Williams, George, III, 1949-
Mark Twain: Jackasshill and the Jumping Frog.
Bibliography: p.
Includes index
1. Mark Twain, 1835-1910. Celebrated jumping frog of Calaveras County. 2. Twain, Mark, 1835-1910--Homes and haunts--California--Calaveras County.
3. Calaveras County (calif.) in literature. 4. Frogs in literature. 5. Authors, American--19th century --Biography. I. Title.
PS1322.C43W55 1988   813'.4   88-1237
ISBN 0-935174-43-5
ISBN 0-935174- 45-1 (pbk.)

Printed in the United States of America

To Doug Kick, Gordon Lane, Jack Curran and Balderdash, in Virginia City, whose humor and goodwill introduced me to the real Nevada. Gentlemen, my thanks.

Table of Contents

Author's Introduction

This is the third book in my *Mark Twain in the West* series. This book is written so it may be read and understood independent of others in the series.

Though most Americans associate Mark Twain with *Tom Sawyer* and the Mississippi River, Samuel Clemens' years in Nevada and California 1861-68, were critical to his development as a person and writer. In the gold and silver mining camps, Clemens turned to writing as a serious career and gathered material he would use in his published works. Clemens adopted his professional name, Mark Twain, not in Missouri as is often believed, but in Nevada Territory in 1863.

Mark Twain and the Jumping Frog of Calaveras County, continues Mark Twain's story from May, 1864 to November, 1865, as Twain leaves Virginia City, Nevada where he has spent twenty-one months as a reporter for the *Daily Territorial Enterprise*. Having won a controversial reputation as a humorist, Mark Twain moves to San Francisco where he continues newspaper reporting, becomes frustrated with the grinding work and concentrates on freelance writing.

Following difficulties in San Francisco, Twain retreats to the Sierra foothills where he discovers the tale of "Jim Smiley and His Jumping Frog." Twain's version, published in November, 1865, earns Mark Twain his first national recognition and launches him on his long career as America's foremost author and humorist of the time.

In writing this book, I have relied on these primary sources: Mark Twain's lettters and notebooks, his published Western writings in the Virginia City *Territorial Enterprise*, *The Californian*, the *Golden Era*, the San Francisco *Morning Call*, and the recollections, letters and journals of those who knew Mark Twain in the West.

Secondary sources I have used are Mark Twain's published works, primarily *Roughing It* and *The Autobiography of*

Mark Twain, which are at times unreliable due to Twain's wonderful imagination, his need to exaggerate and his sometimes faulty memory.

Readers may learn more about Mark Twain's life in the West through other books in this series. The first, *Mark Twain: His Adventures at Aurora and Mono Lake*, tells about Clemens' arrival in Nevada Territory in August, 1861 and his life as a silver miner at Aurora, Nevada from April to October, 1862.

The second, *Mark Twain: His Life In Virginia City, Nevada*, picks up the story in October, 1862, and details Mark Twain's stay in Virginia City where he reported for the *Territorial Enterprise* until May, 1864. While in Virginia City, Clemens adopted his pen name, Mark Twain.

On The Road With Mark Twain In California and Nevada, is a traveler's guide to historic places where Twain lived, wrote, lectured, fished and camped.

Readers may use the Order Form at the end of this book to order autographed copies by mail. Or use our web site to order books. **www.autographed-books.com**

But he knows the way that I take; when he has tested me, I will come forth as gold.   Job 23:10

...You remember the one gleam of jollity that shot across our dismal sojourn in the rain and mud of Angel's Camp. I mean that day we sat around the tavern stove and heard that chap tell about the frog and how they filled him with shot. And you remember how we quoted from the yarn and laughed over it out there on the hillside while you and dear old Stoker panned and washed. I jotted the story down in my notebook that day and would have been glad to get ten or fifteen dollars for it. I was just that blind. But then we were so hard up! I published that story and it became widely known in America, India, China, England, and the reputation it made for me has paid me thousands and thousands of dollars since.

Mark Twain, from a letter to Jim Gillis, January 26, 1870

Mark Twain about 1863 at the age of twenty-eight. Photograph was taken in San Francisco. Photo courtesy of the Mark Twain Project, University of California, Berkeley.

CHAPTER ONE

Mark Twain Leaves Virginia City For San Francisco

"Mark Twain" was not born in Hannibal, Missouri as most of us have been taught. "Mark Twain" was born amidst the bitter odors of whisky, gin and beer in John Piper's bar, in Virginia City, Nevada, then a rip-roaring, take-your-life-in-your-hands, silver mining town atop the rugged Washoe Mountians south of Reno. Piper's "Old Corner Saloon" was the hangout for Sam Clemens and other newspaper reporters and printers who daily ground out Virginia City's several newspapers. The Bohemian crowd gathered in Piper's bar after they put their papers to bed or at "coffee breaks" during the day which were frequent and necessary. Clemens apparently had the habit of going into the bar with one other friend. Clemens would order drinks for himself and his pal and ask Piper to "mark twain," meaning mark two drinks on the chalk board on the wall behind the bar, where Piper kept track of his customers' tabs. Clemens' friends soon nicknamed him "Mark Twain;" Clemens began using the pseudonym shortly after in January, 1863.

Clemens had more or less stumbled into his new career as a reporter for the *Territorial Enterprise* at Virginia City, then the leading newspaper on the West Coast. He was not entirely unprepared for the job. Clemens became familiar with newspaper work at an early age. At thirteen, following the death of his father, Clemens was taken out of school and made a printer's apprentice at the local newspaper in order to help support his family. He learned to set type, to print and became familiar with newspaper work.

Clemens continued educating himself through serious reading. By fifteen he had read the entire Bible and many of the works of Cervantes, Dickens, Goldsmith and Hood. After he found a page from a book about Joan of Arc in the street, Clemens developed a serious interest in history. Clemens was highly curious, had a precocious understanding both of words and human nature and he was a good speller.

He began writing, largely to amuse himself and by seventeen managed to publish a story in an Eastern magazine. After completing his apprenticeship, Clemens worked for two of his brother Orion's newspapers as a printer and editor and occasionally wrote humorous articles in which he made fun of local characters.

When he turned eighteen, Clemens began travelling throughout eastern America where he found newspaper work as a printer and typesetter. During this time he wrote travel articles for several newspapers.

In 1857, at twenty-one, Clemens left newspaper work and spent the next four years as a steamboat pilot on the Mississippi. Had the Civil War not disrupted river traffic in the spring of 1861, Clemens may have remained a river pilot. But with the

Orion Clemens, Sam's older brother, whose appointment as
Secretary of Nevada Territory in 1861, led Sam to go West.
Photo from author's collection.

closure of free river traffic, Clemens was suddenly out of a good paying job.

That August, at twenty-five, Clemens moved on to Carson City, with his older brother, Orion [pronounced Or-ee-un] who had been appointed Secretary of Nevada Territory. Sam hoped to become Orion's secretary; but when he learned his pay would be deducted from Orion's meager salary he decided to try something else.

Clemens then turned his interest to mining. Northwestern Nevada Territory was at this time in a frenzy of mining activity due to the huge strikes of gold and silver discovered at Virginia City, 15 miles northeast of Carson City. Clemens became infected with the madness and roared off on a wild goose chase to Unionville in December, 1861, followed by a six month stint at Aurora from April to October, 1862. Both trips were costly and unsuccessful.

Cooped up in his cabin at Aurora during the spring snows, Clemens began writing humorous letters about the trials and tribulations of a hardluck miner. Clemens signed the letters "Josh" and sent them to the *Territorial Enterprise* in Virginia City where they were published. Editor Joe Goodman was impressed by the "Josh" letters and believed the writer was worth cultivating. Goodman was at this time looking for someone to take Dan De Quille's place in the fall of 1862 as a local reporter. "Josh" seemed a likely replacement. Goodman offered Clemens the reporter position in July, 1862; Clemens accepted. The following October, somewhat reluctantly, Clemens left Aurora for Virginia City. [For more on Mark Twain at Aurora, read the author's, *Mark Twain: His Adventures at Aurora and Mono Lake.*]

Twain's stay on the *Enterprise* was his first full time writing job. Ironically, it was a job he had not actively pursued,

Piper's Opera House on "B" Street, Virginia City. This is the third version, built after the second opera house burned in 1883. At this site in 1862 was located Piper's "Old Corner Saloon," where Sam Clemens drank with other newspapermen and where he was first named "Mark Twain" by his friends. Dan De Quille and Twain lived in the Meyers Building about 100 yards north of here. The building no longer exists. Larry Tanner photo.

yet it had a profound effect on his life. Goodman was a very positive influence on Clemens' creative writing in that he gave Clemens a free hand in his reporting. For twenty-one months, Clemens raked the town for news and wrote it up in a loose, clever style readers found entertaining. Mark Twain's *Enterprise* columns were not bland pieces of news. Instead they were often a budding genius' subjective interpretations of events colored by his wit, wisdom and insight. Through Twain's published hoaxes—one, a gruesome tale about a crazed man who murdered his family with an axe and then slit his own throat, Mark Twain won a controversial reputation in Nevada and on the Coast.

Twain's relationship with Dan De Quille was also an important influence on Clemens' writing during this time. De Quille was at this time an experienced reporter and a popular humorist on the West Coast. Not only did the two men work together, they were roommates and became good friends. De Quille taught Twain the ropes as local reporter on the *Enterprise* and encouraged his humorous writing.

Twain's work as a reporter for the *Territorial Enterprise* met several of his needs and made the job—at least in Virginia City— well suited for him: It enabled him to be involved with others, from the rich banker to the hard rock miner. It appealed to his curiousity and his need for new experiences. Most importantly, it offered him the opportunity to test the waters with his humorous writing on an audience. The response was positive and encouraging; in Virginia City Mark Twain won his first notoriety as a humorous writer.

A number of circumstances and events eventually led Twain to leave Virginia City at the end of May, 1864. For the most part, he was simply fed up with the isolated mining town and fed up with being in one place for so long. In a letter to his brother a few days before leaving Virgnia City, Twain wrote, "...Washoe

[Nevada Territory] has long since grown irksome to us, & we [Steve Gillis and Twain] want to leave it... " [Letter to Orion Clemens, May 26, 1864]

Besides it was spring, and it seemed with each spring, Twain got the urge to travel. He wrote of leaving Virginia City,

I began to get tired of staying in one place so long. There was no longer satisfying variety in going down to Carson [City] to report the proceedings of the legislature once a year, and horse races and pumpkin shows once in three months...I wanted to see San Francisco. I wanted to go somewhere. I wanted—I did not know what I wanted. I had the "spring fever" and wanted a change, principally, no doubt.

Roughing It, Chapter 55

Besides his desires for travel and greater success, something else had happened. One evening after Twain and Dan De Quille had been out drinking, they went down to the *Enterprise* offices. There while drunk, Twain wrote a scathing article about a group of Carson City ladies whom he mistakenly believed had misappropriated donations from the Sanitary Fund, a charity which helped wounded soldiers. Twain never intended the article to be published but mistakenly left it on the printer's table. The printer, believing the article was meant for publication, printed it in the following day's paper.

The Carson ladies were furious when the article appeared. They demanded to know who the author was and asked for an apology. Twain was sorry the article had been mistakenly published; he apologized publicly and privately. Still, the ruckus got so bad, one woman's husband went hunting for Twain with a gun.

In addition, Twain, who had become editor in Joe Goodman's absence, wrote a series of editorials in which he accused James Laird, editor of a rival paper, of his ungenerous support of the Sanitary Fund. Twain and Laird spit a series of heated letters back and forth in their papers. Hostilities reached a pitch when Twain called Laird, "an unmitigated liar," and challenged Laird to a duel. Dueling and challenges to duel were against Nevada law. A friend suggested it was in Twain's best interest to leave Virginia City until the dust settled.

For these reasons, on May 29, 1864, Mark Twain boarded the stage for San Francisco with Steve Gillis and Joe Goodman. Twain wrote of leaving Virginia City:

It was not without regret that I took a last look at the tiny flag (it was thirty-five feet long and ten feet wide) fluttering like a lady's handkerchief from the top most peak of Mt. Davidson, two thousand feet above Virginia's roofs, and felt that doubtless I was bidding a permanent farewell to a city which had afforded me the most vigorous enjoyment of my life I had ever experienced.

Roughing It, Chapter 55

Though at the time he said he would never return to Virginia City, he returned twice, after he had earned greater notoriety in San Francisco. [For more on Mark Twain in Virginia City, read the author's, *Mark Twain: His Life In Virginia City, Nevada.*]

Years later, Steve Gillis recalled their leaving Virginia City that day:

...when the stage left next morning for San Francisco we were on the outside seat. Joe Goodman had returned by this time

and agreed to accompany us as far as Henness Pass. We were all in good spirits and glad we were alive, so Joe did not stop when he got to Henness Pass, but kept on. Now and then he would say, "Well, I had better be going back pretty soon," but went with us clear to San Francisco, and we had a royal good time all the way. I never knew any series of duels to close so happily.

In 1911, Joe Goodman told Twain's biographer, Albert Bigelow Paine, "We all sat on a seat behind the driver on a Concord Coach. I intended to go only a little way out... but the company was too good and I kept clear on to San Francisco." Arriving in San Francisco, Twain, took a room at the Occidental Hotel, a place he considered an oasis. He wrote,

To a Christian who has toiled months and months in Washoe; [Nevada Territory] *whose hair bristles from a bed of sand, and whose soul is caked with a cement of alkali dust; whose nostrils know no perfume but the rank odor of sagebrush—and whose eyes know no landscape but barren mountains and desolate plains; where the winds blow, and the sun blisters, and the broken spirit of the contrite heart finds joy and peace only in Limberger cheese and lager beer—unto such a Christian, verily the Occidental Hotel is Heaven on the half shell. He may even secretly consider it to be Heaven on the entire shell, but his religion teaches a sound Washoe Christian that it would be sacrilege to say it.*

Golden Era, June 26, 1864

In comparison to Virginia City, which was an isolated mining town in a barren desert region, Twain found San Francisco invigorating. It had a population of over 130,000; there were parks, fine restaurants, hundreds of saloons, billiard parlours, high class hotels, many entertaining diversions—musical shows, plays, operas. San Francisco was a seaport more in touch with the outside world; therefore it had greater cultural activities. The weather was temperate and there was greenery, so lacking in Nevada. Finally, San Francisco was next to the Pacific Ocean where there was both the water and the shipping industry that Twain liked being near.

While reporting in Virginia City, Twain made several trips to San Francisco where he met and became friends with San Franciscan writers and publishers. As early as September, 1863, Twain was submitting articles for the *Golden Era*, a San Franciscan literary journal. The publication of these articles throughout 1863 and 64 combined with Twain's *Enterprise* reputation enabled him to land a job with the San Francisco *Morning Call*.

Although Twain initially intended to stay in San Francisco a month, during which time he hoped to sell his Hale and Norcross mining stock and return to the East, by June 6, Twain was working full time for the San Francisco *Call*, as its "local items" reporter. Steve Gillis was hired as a compositor and printer.

As the *Call's* only reporter, Twain worked from early morning until late at night with a regular beat that included the courts, the police station, and local news. It was monotonous and dull work for a man with great imagination. Twain was paid $40 a week, good pay for the time.

Reporting for the *Call* was not easy for Twain. Unlike working for Joe Goodman and the *Enterprise*, where Twain roamed where he pleased and wrote what he wanted—whether invented or not, George Barnes, the *Call's* editor and co-owner, wanted straight reporting, "just the facts." Twain preferred to interpret events in his own humorous and exaggerated manner.

18

Joe Goodman, the young editor of the *Territorial Enterprise*, who believed in Sam Clemens and gave him his first full time writing job. From the author's collection.

Although the *Call* folks were at first pleased to have a writer with Twain's reputation on their paper, it wasn't long before George Barnes realized that Twain was not the writer his newspaper needed. Twain was not permitted the professional courtesy of a by-line and his humorous views of life and events, expressed in his local news columns were not appreciated.

In his *Autobiography*, Twain told of his frustration reporting for the *Call* :

> After leaving Nevada I was a reporter on the Morning Call *of San Francisco. I was more than that—I was* the *reporter. There was no other. There was enough work for one and a little over, but not enough for two—according to Mr. Barnes's idea, and he was the proprietor and therefore better situated to know about it than other people.*
>
> *By nine in the morning I had to be at the police court for an hour and make a brief history of the squabbles of the night before. They were usually between Irishmen and Irishmen, and Chinamen and Chinamen, with now and then a squabble between the two races for a change. Each day's evidence was substantially a duplicate of the evidence of the day before, therefore the daily performance was killingly monotonous and wearisome...Next we visited the higher courts and made notes of the decisions which had been rendered the day before. All the courts came under the head of "regulars." They were sources of reportorial information which never failed. During the rest of the day we raked the town from end to end, gathered such material as we might, wherewith to fill our required column—and if there were no fires to report we started some.*
>
> *At night we visited the six theaters, one after another: seven nights in the week, three hundred and sixty-five nights in the year. We remained in each of those places five minutes, got*

Territorial Enterprise Building, "C" Street, Virginia City,
where Mark Twain wrote from August, 1863 to May, 1864.
Author's photo.

the merest passing glimpse of play and opera, and with that for a text we "wrote up" those plays and operas, as the phrase goes, torturing our souls every night from the beginning of the year to the end of it in the effort to find something to say about those performances which we had not said a couple of hundred times before...

After having been hard at work from nine or ten in the morning until eleven at night scraping material together, I took the pen and spread this muck out in words and phrases and made it cover as much acreage as I could. It was fearful drudgery, soulless drudgery, almost destitute of interest. It was awful slavery for a lazy man, and I was born lazy. I am no lazier now than I was forty years ago, but that is because I reached the limit forty years ago...

Despite Barnes' objections, Twain reported the local news the same casual and humorous way he had on the *Enterprise*. Twain got away with it only because he wrote his columns close to deadline and Barnes had little time to review and edit them. For instance, while reporting an accident caused by the driver's fondness for hard liquor, Twain wrote:

A pile of miscellaneous articles was found heaped up at a late hour last night away down somewhere in Harrison street, which attracted the notice of numbers of passers-by, and divers attempts were made to analyze the same without effect, for the reason that no one could tell where to begin, or which one was on top. Two Special Policemen dropped in just then and solved the difficulty, showing a clean inventory of one horse, one buggy, two men and an indefinite amount of liquor. The liquor couldn't be got at to be gauged, consequently the proof of it couldn't be told; the men, though, were good proof that the liquor was there, for they were as drunk as Bacchus and his brother. A fight had been on hand somewhere, and one of the men had been close to it, for his face was painted up in various hues, sky-blue and crimson being prominent. The order of the buggy was inverted, and the horse beyond realizing sense of his condition. The men went with the animal to the station-house, and the animal, with attachments, being set to rights, ambled off to a livery stable on Kearny street.

Sundries, August 13, 1864, *Call*

Even with such a deadly event as an earthquake, Twain found something humorous to say. When an earthquake hit San Francisco, instead of reporting the flat details of the event, Twain wrote it up like this:

...Last night, at twenty minutes to eleven, the regular semi-monthly earthquake, due the night before, arrived twenty-four hours behind time, but it made up for the delay in uncommon and altogether unnecessary energy and enthusiasm. The first effort was so gentle as to move the inexperienced stranger to the expression of contempt... but the second was calculated to move him out of his boots...Up in the third story of this building the sensation we experienced was as if we had been sent for and were mighty anxious to go. The house seemed to waltz from side to side with a quick motion, suggestive of sifting corn meal through a sieve; afterward it rocked grandly to and fro like a prodigious cradle, and in the meantime several persons started downstairs to see if there were anybody in the street so timid as to be frightened at a mere earthquake. The third shock was not important, as compared with the stunner that had just preceded it. That second shock drove people out of the theatres by dozens.

At the Metropolitan, we are told that Franks, the comedian, had just come on the stage... and was about to express the unbounded faith he had in May; he paused until the jarring had subsided, and then improved and added force to the text by exclaiming, "It will take more than an earthquake to shake my faith in that woman!" And in that, Franks achieved a sublime triumph over the elements, for he "brought the house down," and the earthquake couldn't.

In one of his more humorous items, Twain reconstructs the police court testimony of a local businessman, his wife and another woman. Watch how Twain turns an ordinary court case into an entertaining drama:

Lena Kahn, otherwise known as Mother Kahn, or the Kahn of Tartary, who is famous in this community for the Police Court as a place of recreation, was on hand there again yesterday morning. She was mixed up in a triangular row, [fight] the sides of the triangle being Mr. Oppenheim, Mrs. Oppenheim, and herself. It appeared from the evidence that she formed the base of the triangle—which is to say, she was at the bottom of the row, and struck the first blow. Moses Levi, being sworn, said he was in the neighborhood, and heard Mrs. Oppenheim scream; knew it was her by the vicious expression she always threw into her screams; saw the defendant (her husband) go into the Tartar's house and gobble up the partner of his bosom and his business, and rescue her from the jaws of destruction (meaning Mrs. Kahn,) and bring her forth to sport once more——. At this point the lawyer turned off Mr. Levi's gas, which seemed to be degenerating into poetry, and asked him what his occupation was? The Levite said he drove an express wagon. The lawyer— with that sensitiveness to the slightest infringement of the truth, which is so becoming to the profession—inquired severely if he did not sometimes drive the horses also! The wretched witness, thus detected before the multitude in his deep-laid and subtle prevarication, hung his head in silence. His evidence could no longer be respected, and he moved away from the stand...Mrs. Oppenheim next came forward and gave a portion of her testimony in damaged English, and the balance in dark and mysterious German. In the English glimpses of her story it was discernible that she had innocently tresspassed upon the domain of the Khan, and had been rudely seized upon in such a manner as to make her arm blue, (she turned up her sleeve and showed the Judge,) and the bruise had grown worse since that day, until at last it was tinged with a ghastly green, (she turned up her sleeve again for impartial judicial inspection,) and instantly after receiving this affront, so humiliating to one of gentle blood, she had been set upon without cause or provocation, and thrown upon the floor and "Licked." This last expression possessed a charm for Mrs. Oppenheimer, that no persuasion of Judge or lawyers could induce her to forego, even for the sake of bringing her wrongs into a stronger light...She said the Khan had licked her, and she stuck to it and reiterated with unflinching firmness...she relapsed at last into hopeless German again, and retired within the lines. Mr. Oppenheim then came forward and remained under fire for fifteen minutes, during which time he made it as plain as the disabled condition of his Engligh would permit him to do, that he was not in anywise to blame...that his wife went out after a warrant for the arrest of the Kahn; that she stopped to "make it up" with the Kahn, and the redoubtable Kahn tackled her; that he was dry-nursing the baby at the time, and when he heard his wife scream, he suspected with a sagacity that did him credit, she wouldn't have "hollered 'dout dere was someding de matter;" therefore he piled the child up in a corner *remote from danger, and moved upon the works of the Tartar; she had waltzed into the wife and finished her...*

The Kahn of Tartary, June 29, 1864, *Call*

Both the Kahn and Mrs. Oppenheim were fined $20 each and let go.

In July, Twain and Steve Gillis moved into a rooming house in or near Chinatown. Occasionally they enjoyed raising hell. July 15, 1864, Twain wrote Dan De Quille and gave him an exaggerated account of what their landlady thought of them:

Steve & I have moved our lodgings. Steve did not tell his folks he had moved, & the other day his father went to our room, & finding it locked, he hunted up the old landlady (French-woman,) & asked her where those young men were. She didn't know who he was, & she got her gun off without mincing matters. Said she—"They are gone, thank God—& I hope I may never see them again. I did not know anything about them, or they never should have entered this house. Do you know, Sir, (dropped her voice to a ghastly confidential tone,) they were a couple of desperate characters from Washoe—gamblers & murderers of the very worst description! I never saw such a countenance as the smallest one had on him. They just took the premises, & lorded it over everything—they didn't care a snap for the rules of the house. One night when they were carrying on in their room with some more roughs, my husband went up to remonstrate with them, & that small man told him to take his head out of the door (pointing a revolver,) because he wanted to shoot in that direction. O, I never saw such creatures. Their room was never vacant long enough to be cleaned up—one of them always went to bed at dark & got up at sunrise, & the other went to bed at sun-rise

& got up at dark—& if the chamber-man disturbed them they would just set up in bed & level a pistol at him & tell him to get scarce! They used to bring loads of beer bottles up at midnight, & get drunk, & shout & fire off their pistols in the room, & throw their empty bottles out of the window at the Chinamen below. You'd hear them count One—two—three—fire! & then you'd hear the bottles crash on the China roofs & see the poor Chinamen scatter like flies. O, it was dreadful! They kept a nasty foreign sword & any number of revolvers & bowie knives in their room, & I know that small one must have murdered lots of people. They always had women running to their room—sometimes in broad daylight—bless you, they didn't care. They had no respect for God, man, or the devil. Yes, Sir, they are gone, & the good God was kind to me when He sent them away!"

There, now—what in the hell is the use of wearing away a life-time in building up a good name, if it is to be blown away at a breath by an ignorant foreigner who is ignorant of the pleasant little customs that adorn & beautify a state of high civilization?

The old man told Steve all about it in his dry, unsmiling way, & Steve laughed himself sick over it.

...But don't I want to go to Asia, or somewhere—Oh no, I guess not. I have got the "Gypsy" only in a mild form. It will kill me yet, though.

Looking for ways to increase his income and settle loose ends in Virginia City, September 17, Twain wrote Dan De Quille:

If you will buy my furniture at $55, I'll send you a bill of sale, & then you can sell it to somebody who will suit you better as a bedfellow than [George] *Dawson.*

If you consent, go to Paxton & Thornburgh, Bankers, &

assume a debt I owe them of $55, (provided Harry Blodgett has not already paid it,) & write me a word & the bill of sale shall go up by return mail. Mr Daggett cannot prove that I owe him a cent, & of course he cannot hold my furniture.

Put. has gone back to Sac. [Sacramento] Say, look in Cohen's notary book, & tell me how much money he has received from the first beginning. His book is open to inspection by anybody. All well. Give our love to old Joe & Dennis [Owners of the Enterprise] . I don't work after 6 in the evening, now on the "Call." I got disgusted with night work.

By mid-September, Twain was burned-out working day and night for the *Call.* He told Barnes he would no longer work at night and wrote his mother and sister about his decision September 25:

I am taking life easy, now, and I mean to keep it up for awhile. I don't work at night any more. I told the "Call" folks to pay me $25 a week and let me work only in daylight. So I get up at 10 in the morning, & quit work at 5 or 6 in the afternoon...I have engaged to write for the new literary paper—the "Californian"—same pay I used to receive on the "Golden Era"—one article a week, fifty dollars a month. I quit the "Era," long ago. It wasn't high-toned enough. I thought that whether I was a literary "jackleg" or not, I wouldn't class myself with that style of people, anyhow. The "Californian" circulates among the highest class of the community, and is the best weekly literary paper in the United States—and I suppose I ought to know.

The Californian, was a mixture of magazine and literary journal started by Bret Harte and a partner in May, 1864. Harte was the major contributor and the editor. Harte, who worked for

The International Hotel in Virginia City at the northwest corner of Union and "C" streets at about the time Mark Twain lived in Virginia City. Twain and Dan De Quille had an apartment on "B" Street a few doors down from the International, then one of the finest hotels west of the Mississippi. Photo from the author's collection.

the U.S. Mint in San Francisco, had an office in the Mint Annex. The *Call's* offices were located in the same building on the third floor. The new brick building was at 612 Commercial Street.

Working and writing in the same building, Harte and Twain discovered each other. Though having vastly different natures, they became friends. When each was free, they would spend time together in Harte's office or at a nearby saloon going over each others' writings.

Harte was then the more experienced writer and took an interest in Twain. Harte encouraged Twain in his writing endeavors and taught him how to improve his rough Western humor so that it might reach a wider audience. Though in later years Twain held Harte in contempt for the way Harte neglected his wife and family, during the early years of their friendship Twain credited Harte with having tutored him toward his first national success.

By September 25, Twain and Gillis had moved their lodgings seven times. By October, he would settle on a "...little quiet street," that was "...full of gardens & shrubbery, & there are none but dwelling houses in it." [letter September 25, 1864] This lodging house was at 32 Minna Street. [*San Francisco directory*]

Though now working fewer hours for the *Call*, Twain became increasingly bored and frustrated with his job. George Barnes wanted a consistent nuts-and-bolts reporter who would collect the local news and write it up flatly. Twain used the local news as a means of expressing his humor and perspective. It was clear to Barnes, and becoming clearer to Twain, that he was unsuited for the work.

Additionally, Barnes limited the subjects Twain could write about and have published in the *Call*. His humor and satires were not greatly appreciated. Though Twain managed to sneak in a satire like, *"What A Sky-Rocket Did,"* which poked fun at a former San Franciscan supervisor, such outlets for his satire in the *Call* were few. George Barnes wanted his sluggish reporter to simply get "the facts."

Highly sensitive political articles were also forbidden by Barnes. One day Twain observed a gang chasing and stoning a Chinaman while a policeman stood by and did nothing. The sight outraged Twain. He wrote a fiery article about the incident and anxiously looked for its publication. But editor George Barnes had different ideas about the article. Twain wrote in his *Autobiography* :

One Sunday afternoon I saw some hoodlums chasing and stoning a Chinaman who was heavily laden with the weekly wash of his Christian customers, and I noticed that a policeman was observing this performance with an amused interest—nothing more. He did not interfere. I wrote up the incident with considerable warmth and holy indignation. Usually I didn't want to read in the morning what I had written the night before; it had come from a torpid heart. But this item had come from a live one. There was fire in it and I believed it was literature—and so I sought for it in the paper the next morning with eagerness. It wasn't there. It wasn't there the next morning, nor the next. I went up to the composing room and found it tucked away among condemned matter on the standing galley. I asked about it. The foreman said Mr. Barnes had found it in a galley proof and ordered its extinction. And Mr. Barnes furnished his reasons— either to me or to the foreman, I don't remember which; but they were commercially sound. He said that the Call *was like the New York* Sun *of that day: it was the washerwoman's paper—that is, it was the paper of the poor; it was the only cheap paper. It gathered its livelihood from the poor and must respect their*

*prejudices or perish. The Irish were the poor. They were the stay
and support of the* Morning Call; *without them the* Morning Call
*could not survive a month—and they hated Chinamen. Such an
assault as I had attempted could rouse the whole Irish hive and
seriously damage the paper. The* Call *could not afford to publish
articles criticizing hoodlums for stoning...*

*...I was loftier forty years ago than I am now and I felt
deep shame in being situated as I was—slave of such a journal as
the* Morning Call. *If I had been still loftier I would have thrown
up my berth and gone out and starved, like any other hero. But
I had never had any experience. I had dreamed heroism, like
everybody, but I had no practice and I didn't know how to begin.
I couldn't bear to begin with starving. I had already come near
to that once or twice in my life and got no real enjoyment out of
remembering about it. I knew I couldn't get another berth if I
resigned...Therefore I swallowed my humiliation and stayed
where I was...I continued my work but I took not the least interest
in it, and naturally there were results.*

In early articles like this about the mistreatment of the
Chinese, Mark Twain showed his deep and natural sympathy for
the low and downtrodden. His compassion for others would be
the impetus for much of his later serious work like *Huckleberry
Finn.*

Barnes' refusal to publish Twain's Chinese article was
the last straw. Despite his fear of unemployment, Twain quit the
Call around October 11. He admitted he wasn't totally blame-
less. In the last weeks of reporting he had,

*....neglected my duties and became about as worthless, as
a reporter for a brisk newspaper. And at last one of the
proprietors took me aside, with a charity I still remember with*

considerable respect, and gave me the opportunity to resign my berth and so save myself the disgrace of dismissal.

Roughing It, Chapter 58

Years later, George Barnes remembered his heart to heart talk with Twain:

"Mark, do you know what I think about you as a local reporter?"

"Well, what's your thought?"

"That you are out of your element in the routine of the position, that you are capable of better things in literature."

Mark looked up with a queer twinkle in his eye.

"Oh, ya-a-s, I see. You mean to say I don't suit you."

"Well, to be candid, that's about the size of it."

"Ya-a-s. Well, I'm surprised you didn't find out five months ago."

There was a hearty laugh. He was told his unfitness for the place was discovered soon after he entered on it...

Clemens of the "Call," Mark Twain In San Francisco

George Barnes recalled Twain was a, "good general writer and correspondent, ... [but he] made but an indifferent reporter. He only played at itemizing." He, "parted from THE CALL people on the most friendly terms... admitting his reportorial shortcomings and expressing surprise they were not sooner discovered." ["Mark Twain. As He Was Known during His Stay on the Pacific Slope," George E. Barnes, *Morning Call,* April 17, 1887.]

Two things had helped Twain quit the *Call*. One, he was writing articles for the *Californian*, which paid him well, allowed him to express himself, required less work, and provided him with the prestige he desired. Second, Twain was toying with the idea of writing a book, and naturally, he would need time for that. He wrote his brother Orion, September 28:

I <u>would</u> commence on my book, but (mind, this is a secret, & must not be mentioned,) Steve & I are getting things ready for his wedding, which will take place on the 24th Oct. He will marry Miss Emmelina Russ, who is worth $100,000, & what is much better, is a good, sensible girl & will make an excellent wife. Of course I shall "stand up" with Steve, at the nuptials, as chief mourner. We shall take a bridal tour of a week's duration...

I only get $12 an article for the Californian but you see it makes my wages up to what they were on the Call, when I worked at night, & the paper has an exalted reputation in the east, & is liberally copied from by papers like the Home Journal...

Well Mollie [Orion's wife] I <u>do</u> go to church. How's that? As soon as this wedding business is over, I believe I will send to you for the files, & begin my book.

Ironically, Twain did not start his book. Nor did Orion send him his "files," a collection of Twain's articles published in Nevada newspapers, which Orion had saved. These articles, and the letters Twain wrote to his mother and sister while living in Nevada and California, would be the basis for parts of Mark Twain's second book, *Roughing It*, which Twain wrote after he left the West for good.

Twain's only income now came from the publication of articles he wrote for *The Californian*. Between November 12 and December 3rd, 1864, Twain published three articles for which he was paid $12 each. Including his partial October *Call* salary, Twain's total income from October 11, to December 3rd, was about $61. It was the least amount of money Twain had made in two years and it bothered him. He wrote of this desperate time:

For two months my sole occupation was avoiding acquaintances; for during that time I did not earn a penny, or buy an article of any kind, or pay my board. I became very adept at "slinking." I slunk from back street to back street, I slunk away from approaching faces that looked familiar, I slunk to my meals, ate them humbly and with a mute apology for every mouthful I robbed my generous landlady of, and at midnight, after wanderings that were but slinkings away from cheerfulness and light, I slunk to my bed. I felt meaner, and lowlier and more despicable than the worms. During all this time I had but one piece of money—a silver ten cent piece—and I held to it and would not spend it on any account, lest the consciousness coming strong upon me that I was entirely penniless, might suggest suicide. I had pawned every thing but the clothes I had on; so I clung to my dime desperately, till it was smooth with handling.

Roughing It, Chapter 59

In late November, Steve Gillis, a small but fierce fighter, was involved in a barroom brawl with Big Jim Casey, a Barbary Coast saloonkeeper. Gillis brained Casey with a beer pitcher and nearly killed him. Gillis was arrested for assault with intent to kill; Twain posted Gillis' $500 bond.

When Casey's condition worsened and it looked like he might die, Gillis figured it was in his best interest to leave San Francisco until the trouble blew over. Gillis returned to Virginia City and went back to work for the *Enterprise*. Gillis' skipping town, left Twain responsible for Gillis' $500 bond. Twain did not have the money and that meant Twain himself might end up in jail.

There is some speculation as to exactly why Twain left San Francisco in December, 1864. Albert Bigelow Paine believed Twain left town both to escape paying Gillis' bond and to avoid trouble with the police following Twain's publication of articles about San Francisco police corruption. However, these articles were not published until October, 1865, long after Twain had returned from Jackass Hill.

Gillis' bond trouble may have been part of Twain's decison to leave. But a lack of income and a need of rest are more plausible reasons. At the time Twain left San Francisco for Jackass Hill, he was nearly broke and needed a place to stay. Twain admitted that he was unable to pay his landlady for room and board. Even after he returned from Jackass Hill, he spent more than a year repaying his past debts.

Besides being broke, Twain was just plain tired. For four months he had worked hard as a reporter for the *Call* . While writing for the *Call*, and for two months afterward, Twain had written a number of articles for literary papers attempting to establish himself as a free-lance writer. After quitting the *Call*, his struggle to earn a living as a free-lance writer and his failure to earn enough to cover living expenses, increased Twain's mental stress. Any serious writer who has pounded out writing daily, foregoing the luxury of a paycheck at the end of the week, understands the horrible burden one feels when he is unable to pay for basic living expenses. Broke, stressed-out and mentally tired, Twain needed a rest.

With all this in mind, Twain's decision to leave town fits his lifelong work pattern: intense periods of work followed by long rests. These rests were often spent travelling.

So it appears, Twain left for Jackass Hill for a combination of reasons: he couldn't afford to pay Steve Gillis' $500 bond and he didn't want to go to jail. He was broke, needed a place to stay, and he needed rest. Jackass Hill was perfect.

"By and by, an old friend of mine, a miner, came down from one of the decayed mining camps of Tuolumne, [County] California, and I went back with him," wrote Twain. [*Roughing It*, Chapter 60] The old friend was Jim Gillis, Steve's brother. Jim Gillis suggested Mark Twain stay with him on Jackass Hill until the San Francisco trouble ended.

Twain left San Francisco around December 1 and arrived on Jackass Hill, December 4. While roaming the Sierra foothills with Jim Gillis in search of gold, Mark Twain unearthed real treasure when he discovered the tale about Jim Smiley and his jumping frog.

Mark Twain was then twenty-nine. By his thirtieth birthday, his version of the jumping frog story would earn him national attention and launch him on his way to becoming America's foremost author and humorist.

Here's how it happened:

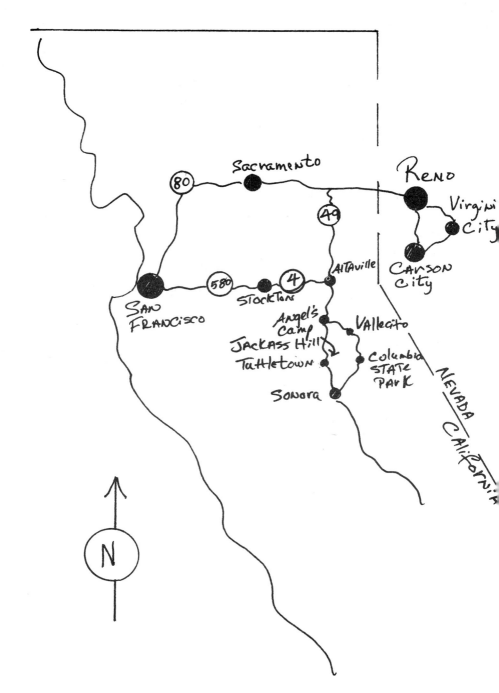

San Francisco at about the time Mark Twain lived there 1864-68. Photo from the author's collection.

CHAPTER TWO

Jackass Hill and Jim Gillis

Jim Gillis' home was a one room plank cabin on Jackass Hill. The Hill was named "Jackass," in the late 1840's because of the large numbers of jackasses that teamsters parked on the Hill on their supply trips to the Mother Lode mining camps.

Jim Gillis, and his partner, Dick Stoker, had mining claims all over the Hill. Today the reddish-brown earth of Jackass is pock-marked with a myriad of bomb-shell holes where the Gillises and Stoker, and miners afterward, dug their "pocket" mines. There are a few mine shafts with the usual piles of rock and sand. But for the most part, miners worked shallow pockets rather than incur the labor, expense and danger of underground mining.

The original Gillis cabin where Mark Twain stayed is gone. It was long gone in 1907 when Albert Bigelow Paine, Twain's first biographer, visited the Hill. Word has it that the cabin fell apart after years of disuse and then burned down entirely around 1900.

Today on Jackass Hill you will find a replica of the original cabin built in 1922 under Billy Gillis' supervision. Billy Gillis had lived in the cabin at the time Twain stayed on Jackass Hill. He led the builders to the original cabin site where they uncovered portions of the foundation. Billy told the builders what the original cabin looked like and a replica was built to his specifications. The Gillis family then donated the cabin and the land it is located on to Tuolumne County.

Gillis and Stoker's one room cabin was about twenty feet long and ten feet wide built in a grove of live oak trees. The cabin actually belonged to Dick Stoker who built it in 1850. At the west end of the dirt floored cabin there was a stone fireplace whose mantel Jim Gillis leaned against while telling his impromptu stories. Twain described Gillis and Stoker's cabin in 1864, "No planking on the floor; old bunks, pans, traps of all kinds—Byron Shakespeare, Bacon, Dickens, & every kind of only first class Literature." [*Notebook 4*]

For years, the replica cabin was left open and visitor's could walk in. Inside the cabin were various personal items belonging to the Gillises: a desk, crude miner's stools, tools, pick-axes and the like. Tourists eventually stole everything from the cabin. A high black iron fence was built around the cabin in the 1980's to keep visitors and thieves out. Most of the Hill today—except where the Mark Twain Cabin stands, is still owned by descendants of the Gillises.

Today, amidst the grove of live oak trees and pines of Jackass Hill, there are a few recently built homes. But the Hill still has that quiet, far away from it all, somewhat lonely feeling it had when Twain lived there. In the early spring, the tall grasses of wild oats are green and the wild flowers splatter their varied colors across the surrounding steep hillsides. In summer the wild oats dry up and the hills become straw colored, spotted with black places where the live oaks stand. The hills remain dead and dry until the winter rains make them green again.

Jackass Hill is on the western slope of the Sierra Nevada mountains, about 100 miles east of San Francisco and 8 miles north of Sonora. Jackass Gulch, more commonly known as Tuttletown, was once the nearest community, about two miles away. Today Tuttletown is just a bend in Highway 49, in a narrow gully thickly enclosed by oak trees and brush. A California historic landmark tells the visitor here was once Tuttletown and "Swerer's store," where Mark Twain traded. All that's left of the store is part of the slab foundation. Today there's a recently built wooden store and a few houses up a canyon.

From western California, the easiest route to Jackass Hill, is to take Highway 4 from Stockton and head east to Altaville. Then head south on Highway 49 eleven miles past Angel's Camp where a side road on the left, or east side, leads one mile up to Jackass Hill and "Mark Twain's Cabin."

Highway 49 winds north and south along the western Sierra foothills through what is known as the California Gold Rush Country or the Mother Lode. Along this popular route were once hundreds of settlements founded after 1848 during the California Gold Rush. Some have disappeared. But many still exist and are new homes for disgruntled city dwellers who have moved here in search of peace and clean air. Gold Rush buildings and houses have been restored and the tiny towns are quaint and attractive.

When Twain visited here in 1864, the Gold Rush had been dead more than a decade. Other mining camps in California and Nevada had drawn most of the living elsewhere. Miners and merchants had left behind clapboard and brick towns like corpses with their hearts cut out. Paint on wooden buildings dried and

Top, allegedly the Gillis-Stoker cabin on Jackass Hill where Mark Twain stayed December 1864 to February 1865. Below, the replica cabin built in the 1920's. Top photo courtesy of Tuolumne County Historical Society.

cracked. Skins of bare wooden buildings burned a deep brown and the boards curled and twisted in the blistering summers. Brick buildings split open and spilled their guts in piles of rubble. Many buildings lost their strength and collapsed from the heat, cold and neglect.

Jackass Gulch (Tuttletown) had become one of those once thriving places that had nearly been deserted when Twain visited. In 1864, Jackass Gulch was no longer a village, just a stone general store, "Swerer's Store," the two story wooden Tuttletown Hotel, built in 1852, and a solitary saloon. First called Mormon Gulch, Jackass Gulch had been established in 1848 at the break of the California Gold Rush. Years after his visit, Mark Twain recalled Jackass Gulch in 1864:

...Jackass Gulch [Tuttletown] *had once been a rich and thriving surface-mining camp. By and by its gold deposits were exhausted; then the people began to go away and the town began to decay, and rapidly; in my time it had disappeared. Where the bank and the city hall and the church and the gambling-dens and the newspaper office and the streets of brick blocks had been, was nothing now but a wide and beautiful expanse of green grass, a peaceful and charming solitude. Half a dozen scattered dwellings were still inhabited and there was still one saloon of a ruined and rickety character struggling for life, but doomed.*

The Autobiography of Mark Twain

Some stubborn souls stayed behind in the lonely settlements of the gold country. Jim Gillis was one.

Jim Gillis [1830-1907] was the eldest of the four Gillis brothers. He was thirty-four when Mark Twain stayed with him at Jackass Hill. Twain was then twenty-nine. Mark Twain wrote

Top, Tuttletown (Jackass Gulch) in the 1920's. Tuttletown
Hotel is on the left, Swerer's store, where Mark Twain and
the Gillises traded is on the right. Below, Swerer's store.
None of these buildings exist today. Photos courtesy of the
Tuolumne County Historical Society.

of Jim Gillis as being an "old friend," at the time he visited Gillis on Jackass Hill. The two likely first met in San Francisco through Steve Gillis.

Jim Gillis was educated at a university according to Twain. Where and for how long is unknown. Gillis appreciated and enjoyed serious literature. He was well read despite his occupation as a hard-luck miner and his isolation in the decayed Mother Lode country. Gillis had a talent with words, a bright imagination and a terrific sense of humor. Twain believed Gillis was a literary genius who could have been a successful humorous writer if he had disciplined himself. Gillis and Twain got along well.

It was Jim Gillis, who, while Twain stayed with him, improvised the story of Dick Baker and his cat, Tom Quartz, one evening by the fireplace. Mark Twain told his own version in *Roughing It*, Chapter 61. Twain based the character Dick Baker on Gillis' roommate, Dick Stoker, Jacob Richard Stoker [1818-96] a forty-six year old bachelor whom Twain described in *Roughing It* as, "...one of the gentlest spirits that ever bore its patient cross in a weary exile...grave and simple...gray as a rat, earnest, thoughtful, slenderly educated, slouchily dressed and clay-soiled, but his heart was finer metal than any gold his shovel ever brought to light—that any, indeed, that ever was mined or minted." Gillis also created the drama, " The Tragedy of the Burning Shame," which the boys acted out in the cabin .

During Twain's three month stay, Billy Gillis, Jim's youngest brother, also lived in the cabin.

Twain admired the Gillises for their courage and character. This he believed was inherited from their father, Major Angus Gillis who had served as a soldier under William Walker in Central America. Twain wrote of Major Gillis in his *Autobiography* :

To say that a man was a major under Walker and came out of that struggle ennobled by Walker's praise is to say that the major was not merely a brave man but that he was brave to the very utmost limit of that word...The father had received a bullet through the eye. The old man—for he was an old man at the time—wore spectacles, and the bullet and one of the glasses went into his skull, and the bullet remained there—but often, in after years, when I boarded in the old man's home in San Francisco, whenever he became emotional I used to see him shed tears and glass, in a way that was infinitely moving...in the course of time he exuded enough to set up a spectacle shop...

In 1865, Twain lived with Angus Gillis at 44 Minna Street, in San Francisco. [*San Francisco directory, 1865*]

Though Mark Twain lived with Jim Gillis a mere three months, for more than four decades afterward, Jim was a person Twain recalled with love. Perhaps this was because Jim was part of Twain's free living, adventurous years in Nevada and California which Mark Twain fondly recalled when old. More importantly, Jim Gillis was the leading character in Twain's stay in the California Gold Country which led to the discovery of the "Jumping Frog" story, the publication of which launched his international career and eventually earned him thousands of dollars.

In May, 1907, learning that Jim Gillis had died, Mark Twain dictated an impassioned remembrance of him for his *Autobiography*. This was forty-three years after his stay on Jackass Hill. The following helps us to understand how greatly Twain admired and loved Jim Gillis. It also tells us what Twain was doing while living on Jackass Hill.

I mourn for Jim. He was a good and steadfast friend, a manly one, a generous one; an honest and honorable man and endowed with a lovable nature. He instituted no quarrels himself but whenever a quarrel was put upon him he was on deck and ready.

I think Jim Gillis was a much more remarkable person than his family and his intimates ever suspected. He had a bright and smart imagination and it was the kind that turns out impromptu work and does it well, does it with easy facility and without previous preparation, just builds a story as it goes along, careless of whither it is proceeding, enjoying each fresh fancy as it flashes from the brain and caring not at all whether the story shall ever end brilliantly and satisfactorily or shan't end at all. Jim was born a humorist and a very competent one. When I remember how felicitous were his untrained efforts, I feel a conviction that he would have been a star performer if he had been discovered and had been subjected to a few years of training with a pen. A genius is not very likely to ever discover himself; neither is he very likely to be discovered by his intimates; they are so close to him that he is out of focus to them and they can't get at his proportions; they cannot perceive there is any considerable difference between his bulk and their own. They can't get a perspective on him and it is only by a perspective that the difference between him and the rest of their limited circle can be perceived.

...I spent three months in the log-cabin home of Jim Gillis and his "pard," Dick Stoker, in Jackass Gulch, that serene and reposeful and dreamy and delicious sylvan paradise...Every now and then Jim would have an inspiration and he would stand up before the great log fire, with his back to it and his hands crossed behind him, and deliver himself of an elaborate impromptu lie— a fairy tale, an extravagant romance—with Dick Stoker as the

Jim Gillis in his fifties, from a photograph of a group of Tuolumne County Pioneers. Photo courtesy of the Tuolumne County Historical Society.

hero of it as a general thing. Jim always soberly pretended that what he was relating was strictly history, veracious history, not romance. Dick Stoker, gray headed and good natured, would sit smoking his pipe and listen with a gentle serenity to these monstrous fabrications and never utter a protest.

In one of my books—Huckleberry Finn, I think—I have used one of Jim's impromptu tales, which he called ""The Tragedy of the Burning Shame." I had to modify it considerable to make it proper for print and this was a great damage. As Jim told it, inventing it as he went along, I think it was one of the most outrageously funny things I have ever listened to. How mild it is in the book and how pale; how extravagant and how gorgeous in the unprintable form! I used another of Jim's impromptus in a book of mine called A Tramp Abroad, a tale of how the poor innocent and ignorant woodpeckers [Blue jays] tried to fill up a house with acorns...I used another of Jim's inventions in one of my books [Roughing It] the story of Jim Baker's cat, the remarkable Tom Quartz. Jim [Dick] Baker was Dick Stoker, of course; Tom Quartz had never existed; there was no such cat, at least outside of Jim Gillis's imagination.

Once or twice Jim's energetic imagination got him into trouble. A squaw came along one day and tried to sell us some wild fruit that looked like large greenages. Dick Stoker had lived in that cabin eighteen years and knew that product was worthless and inedible; but heedlessly and without purpose he remarked that he had never heard of it before. That was enough for Jim. He launched out with fervent praises of that devilish fruit, and the more he talked about it the warmer and stronger his admiration of it grew. He said that he had eaten it a thousands times; that all one needed to do was to boil it with a little sugar and there was nothing on the American continent that would compare with it for deliciousness. He was only talking to hear himself talk; and so

Dick Stoker, from a photograph of early Tuolumne County pioneers. Courtesy of the Tuolumne County Historical Society. **51**

he was...smitten dumb when Dick interrupted him with the remark that if the fruit was so delicious why didn't he invest in it on the spot? Jim was caught but he wouldn't let on; he had gotten himself into a scrape but he was not a man to back down or confess; he pretended that he was only too happy to have this chance to enjoy once more this precious gift of God. Oh, he was a loyal man to his statements! I think he would have eaten that fruit if he known it would kill him. He bought the lot and said airlily and complacently that he was glad enough to have that benefaction, and that if Dick and I didn't want to enjoy it with him we could let it alone—he didn't care.

Then there followed a couple of the most delightful hours I have ever spent. Jim took an empty kerosene can of about a three-gallon capacity and put it on the fire and filled it half full of water and dumped into it a dozen of those devilsih fruits; and as soon as the water came to a good boil he added a handful of brown sugar; as the boiling went on he tested the odious mess from time to time; the unholy vegetables grew softer and softer, pulpier and pulpier, and now he began to make tests with a tablespoon. He would dip out a spoonful and taste it, smack his lips with fictitious satisfaction, remark that perhaps it need a little more sugar—so he would dump in a handful and let the boiling go on a while longer; handful after handful of sugar went in and still the tasting went on for two hours, Stoker and I laughing at him, ridiculing him, deriding him, blackguarding him all the while, and he retained his serenity unruffled.

At last he said the manufacture had reached the right stage, the stage of perfection. He dipped his spoon, tasted, smacked his lips and broke into enthusiasms of grateful joy; then he gave us a taste apiece. From all that we could discover, those tons of sugar had not affected that fruit's malignant sharpness in the least degree. Acid? It was all acid, vindictive acid, uncompro-

mising acid, with not a trace of the modifying sweetness which the sugar ought to have communicated to it and would have communicated to it if that fruit had been invented anywhere outside of perdition. We stopped with that one taste, but that great-hearted Jim, that dauntless martyr, went on sipping and sipping and sipping, and praising and praising and praising and praising, until his teeth and tongue were raw, and Stoker and I nearly dead with gratitude and delight. During the next two days neither food nor drink passed Jim's teeth; so sore were they that they could not endure the touch of anything; even his breath passing over them made them wince; nevertheless he went steadily on voicing his adulations of that brutal mess and praising God. It was an astonishing exhibition of grit, but Jim was like all the other Gillises, he was made of grit.

About once a year he would come down to San Francisco, discard his rough mining costume, buy a fifteen-dollar suit of ready made slops and stride up and down Montgomery Street with his hat tipped over one ear and looking as satisified as a king. The sarcastic stares which the drifting stream of elegant fashion cast upon him did not trouble him; he seemed quite unaware. On one of these occasions Joe Goodman and I and one or two other intimates took Jim up into the Bank Exchange billiard room. It was the resort of the rich and fashionable young swells of San Francisco. The time was ten at night and the twenty tables were all in service, all occupied. We strolled up and down the place to let Jim have a full opportunity to contemplate and enjoy this notable feature of the city.

Every now and then a fashionable young buck dropped a sarcastic remark about Jim and his clothes. We heard these remarks but hoped that Jim's large satisfaction with himself would prevent his discovering that he was the object of them; but that hope failed; Jim presently began to take notice; then he *began to try to catch one of these men in the act of making his remark. He presently succeeded. A large and handsomely dressed young gentleman was the utterer. Jim stepped toward him and came to a standstill, with his chin lifted and his haughty pride exhibiting itself in his attitude and bearing, and said impressively, "That was for me. You must apologize or fight."*

Half a dozen of the neighboring players heard him say it and they faced about and rested the butts of their cues on the floor and waited with amused interests for results. Jim's victim laughed ironically and said, "Oh, is that so? What would happen if I declined?"

"You will get a flogging that will mend your manners."

"Oh, indeed! I wonder if that's so."

Jim's manner remained grave and unruffled. He said, "I challenge you. You must fight me."

"Oh, really! Will you be so good as to name the time?"

"Now."

"This is charming! Weapons?"

"Double-barreled shotguns loaded with slugs; distance thirty feet."

It was high time to interfere. Goodman took the young fool aside and said, "You don't know your man and you are doing a most dangerous thing. You seem to think he is joking but he is not joking, he is not that kind; he's in earnest; if you decline the duel he will kill you where you stand; you must accept his terms and must do it right away, for you have no time to waste; take the duel or apologize. You will apologize, of course, for two reasons: you insulted him when he was not offending you; that is one reason; the other is that you naturally neither want to kill an unoffending man nor be killed yourself. You will apologize and you will let him word the apology; it will be more strong and more uncompromising than any apology that you, even with the most liberal intentions, would be likely to frame."

The man apologized, repeating the words as they fell from Jim's lips—the crowd massed around the pair and listening—and the character of the apology was in strict accordance with Goodman's prediction concerning it.

During the time Twain lived on Jackass Hill, Jim, Billy Gillis and Dick Stoker earned meager livings through "pocket" gold mining.

Twain explained this curious human endeavor in his *Autobiography* :

A "pocket" is a concentration of gold dust in one little spot on a mountainside; it is close to the surface; the rains wash its particles down the mountainside and they spread, fan-shape, wider and wider as they go. The pocket-miner washes a pan of dirt, finds a speck or two of gold in it, makes a step to the right or to the left, washes another pan, finds another speck or two, and goes on washing to the right and to the left until he knows when he has reached both limits of the fan by the best of circumstantial evidence, to wit—that his pan washings furnish no longer the speck of gold. The rest of the work is easy—he washes along up the mountainside, tracing the narrowing fan by his washings, and at last reaches the gold deposit. It may contain only a few hundred dollars, which he can take out with a couple of dips of his shovel; also it may contain a concentrated treasure worth a fortune. It is the fortune he is after and he will seek it with a never-perishing hope as long as he lives.

These friends of mine [Jim Gillis and Dick Stoker] *had been seeking that fortune daily for eighteen years; they had never found it but they were not at all discouraged; they were quite sure they would find it some day. During the three months that I was with them they found nothing, but we had a fascinating and delightful good time trying. Not long after I left, a greaser (Mexican) came loafing along and found a pocket with a hundred and twenty-five thousand dollars in it on a slope which our boys had never happened to explore.*

Of the pocket miners around Jackass Hill, Twain wrote in *Roughing It:*

There are not now more than twenty pocket miners in that entire little region. I think I know every one of them personally. I have known one of them to hunt patiently about the hillsides every day for eight months without finding gold enough to make a snuffbox—his grocery bill running up relentlessly all the time— and then find a pocket and take out of it two thousands dollars in two hours, and go and pay up every cent of his indebtedness, then enter on a dazzling spree that finished the last of his treasure before the night was gone. And the next day he bought his groceries on credit as usual, and shouldered his pan and shovel and went off to the hills hunting pockets again happy and content. This is the most fascinating of all the different kinds of mining, and furnishes a very handsome percentage of victims to the lunatic asylum.

...The hogs are good pocket hunters. All the summer they root around the bushes, and turn up a thousand little piles of dirt, and then the miners long for the rains; for the rains beat upon these little piles and wash them down and expose the gold, possibly right over a pocket. Two pockets were found this way by the same man in one day. One had five thousand dollars in it and the other eight thousand dollars. That man could appreciate it, for he hadn't had a cent for about a year.

Mark Twain tried his hand at pocket mining with Jim, Billy Gillis and Dick Stoker. But he, like the others, was not successful. He wrote:

At the end of two months we had never "struck" a pocket. We had panned up and down the hillsides till they looked plowed like a field; we could have put in a crop of grain, then, but there would have been no way to get it to market. We got many good "prospects", but when the gold gave out in the pan and we dug down, hoping and longing, we found only emptiness— the pocket that should have been there was as barren as our own. At last we shouldered our pans and shovels and struck out over the hills to try new localities. We prospected around Angel's Camp, in Calaveras County, during three weeks, but had no success. Then we wandered on foot among the mountains, sleeping under trees at night, for the weather was mild, but still we remained as centless as the last rose of summer. That is a poor joke, but it is in pathetic harmony with the circumstances, since we were so poor ourselves. In accordance with the custom of the country, our door had always stood open and our board welcome to tramping miners— they drifted along nearly every day, dumped their paust shovels by the threshold, and took "potluck" with us—and now on our tramp we never found cold hospitality.
Our wanderings were wide and in many directions...

Roughing It, Chapter 61

CHAPTER THREE

From Jackass Hill to Angel's Camp

Mark Twain spent December, 1864 with Jim Gillis and Dick Stoker at the Jackass Hill cabin. He wrote,

We lived in a small cabin on a verdant hillside, and there were not five other cabins in view over the wide expanse of hill and forest. Yet a flourishing city of two or three thousand population had occupied this grassy dead solitude during the flush times of twelve or fifteen years before, and where our cabin stood had once been the heart of the teeming hive, the center of the city...The grassy slopes were as green and smooth and desolate of life as if they had never been disturbed. The mere handful of miners still remaining had seen the town spring up, spread, grow, and flourish in its pride; and they had seen it sicken and die, and pass away like a dream. With it their hopes had died, and their zest of life. They had long resigned themselves to their exile and ceased to correspond with their distant friends or turn longing eyes toward their early homes. They had accepted banishment, forgotten the world and been forgotten of the world. They were far from telegraphs and railroads, and they stood, as it were, in a living grave, dead to the events that stirred the globe's great populations, dead to the common interests of men, isolated and outcast from brotherhood with their kind. It was the most singular, and almost the most touching and melancholy exile that fancy can imagine. One of my associates in this locality, for two or three months, was a man who had had a university education; but now for eighteen years he had decayed there by inches, a bearded, rough-clad, clay-stained miner, and at times, among his sighings and soliloquizings, he unconsciously interjected vaguely remembered Latin and Greek sentences—dead and musty tongues, meet vehicles for the thoughts of one whose dreams were all of the past, whose life was a failure; a tired man, burdened with the present and indifferent to the future; a man without ties, hopes, interests, waiting for rest and the end.

Roughing It, Chapter 60

In between pocket mining explorations, the boys walked down the hill to Tuttletown for groceries at Swerer's Store and drinks, conversation and billiards at Tuttletown's one saloon.

Thankfully, Tuttletown did offer Mark Twain one of the things he most enjoyed in life: billiards. Mark Twain was a lifelong billiards fanatic. He would play the game for hours. In one of his offices in later years, he had a billiards table installed. During breaks from writing he would play billiards by himself, or with friends late in the evening. Twain, Jim Gillis and their pocket mining friends had a lot of fun at the worn out billiards table in the Tuttletown saloon. Twain wrote about it in his *Autobiography*,

In its bar was a billiard outfit that was the counterpart of the one in my father-in-law's garret. The balls were chipped, the cloth was darned and patched, the table's surface was undulating and the cues were headless and had the curve of a parenthesis—but the forlorn remnant of marooned miners played games there and those games were more entertaining to look at than a circus and a grand opera combined. Nothing but a quite extraordinary skill could score a carom on that table—a skill that required the nicest estimate of force, distance and how much to allow for the various slants of the table and the other formidable peculiarities and idiosyncrasies furnished by the contradictions of the outfit. Last winter, [winter of 1905-06] ...I saw ...four other billiard champions of world-wide fame contend against each other, and certainly the art and science displayed were a wonder to see; yet I saw nothing there in the way of science and art that was more wonderul than shots which I had seen Texas Tom make on the wavy surface of that poor old wreck in the perishing saloon at Jackass Gulch forty years before. Once I saw Texas Tom make a string of seven points on a single inning!—all calculated shots, and not a fluke or a scratch among them. I often saw him make runs of four, but when he made his great string of seven the boys went wild with enthusiasm and admiration...it might persuade the great experts to discard their own trifling game and bring the Jackass Gulch outfit here and exhibit their skill in a game worth a hundred of the discarded one for profound and breathless interest and for displays of almost superhuman skill.

Most of the time Mark, Jim and Dick hung around the Jackass Hill cabin sharing yarns, reading Byron, Shakespeare,

Dickens and doing odd jobs around the cabin. Twain is said to have spent time reading and writing beneath a large oak tree beside the cabin. The oak tree has since died. A large stump remains near the original cabin site.

Of his life on Jackass Hill, Twain later wrote:

Our clothes were pretty shabby but that was no matter; we were in the fashion; the rest of the slender population were dressed as we were. Our boys hadn't had a cent for several months and hadn't needed one, their credit being perfectly good for bacon, coffee, flour, beans and molasses. If there was any difference, Jim [Gillis] *was the worst dressed of the three of us; if there was any discoverable difference in the matter of age, Jim's shreds were the oldest; but he was a gallant creature and his style and bearing could make any costume regal. One day we were in the decayed and naked and rickety inn when a couple of musical tramps appeared; one of them played the banjo and the other one danced unscientific clog-dances and sang comic songs that made a person sorry to be alive. They passed the hat and collected three or four dimes from the dozen bankrupt pocket-miners present. When the hat approached Jim he said to me, with his fine millionaire air, "Let me have a dollar."*

I gave him a couple halves. Instead of modestly dropping them into the hat, he pitched them into it at the distance of a yard, just as in the ancient novels milord the Duke doesn't hand the beggar a benefaction but "tosses" it to him or flings it at his feet—and it is always a "purse of gold." In the novel, the witnesses are always impressed; Jim's great spirit was the spirit of the novel; to him the half-dollars were a purse of gold; like the Duke he was playing to the gallery, but the parallel ends there. In the Duke's case, the witnesses knew he could afford the purse of gold, and the largest part of their admiration consisted in envy of the man who could throw around purses of gold that fine and careless way. The miners admired Jim's handsome liberality but they knew he couldn't afford what he had done, and that fact modified their admiration. Jim was worth a hundred Bret Harte, for he was a man, and a whole man. In his little exhibition of vanity and pretense he exposed a charactersitic which made him resemble Harte, but the resemblance began and ended there...

The Autobiography of Mark Twain

On New Year's Eve, the boys hiked over Table Mountain to Vallecito, in Calaveras County. Vallecito, Spanish for "little valley," had been a roaring mining camp in the early 1850's. When Twain visited, Vallecito was a quiet town with a general store and a single church. A bell that had been used to call the miners to worship, hung in an old oak tree beside the church. A hillside west of town held the remains of the miners who had died during the early days. Many were Mexican.

Vallecito can be reached today from Angel's Camp or from Columbia, north of Sonora. From Sonora, the trip is 13 miles. Why Jim Gillis and Twain went to Vallecito is uncertain. They may have been on their way to Angel's Camp where Gillis held a pocket mining claim.

What is important about their trip to Vallecito, is that Mark Twain began his fourth notebook there on New Year's Day. Notebook 4 contains brief notes about Twain's stay in the Jackass Hill country and references to stories he would later use in *Roughing It* and other works.

In his first entry of Notebook 4, Twain wrote, "New Year's night 1865, at Vallecito, magnificent lunar rainbow, first appearing at 8PM—moon at first quarter—very light drizzling rain."

A monument to Mark Twain in a park at Angel's Camp, California. Author's photo.

"New Year's night—dream of Jim Townsend..." Twain's dream of Jim Townsend was prophetic. "Lying" Jim Townsend was a journalist and friend of Twain's. The two had met in Virginia City while both worked for the *Enterprise* . Townsend was well known on the West Coast for his tall tales. He had written for the *Golden Era* and several mining camp newspapers.

Scholars have discovered "Lying" Jim Townsend wrote a brief version of the jumping frog story which appeared in the Sonora *Herald* in 1853. Angel's Camp, where Twain would first hear the story of the jumping frog, was but twenty miles from Sonora. After Townsend's publication of the jumping frog story, miners retold it throughout the mining camps until the original source was forgotten. Twain was to rehear Townsend's story in Angel's Camp eleven years after Townsend originally published it.

January 3rd, Twain and Jim Gillis returned to Jackass Hill by making a loop through Angel's Camp, then heading south crossing the Stanislaus River at Robinsons' Ferry. Back on Jackass Hill, the days were spent as before reading and telling each other stories. About this time, Jim Gillis related his impromptu story, "Tragedian & the Burning Shame." Twain made note of the story in his notebook. He would later use a less profane, version in *Huckleberry Finn.*

Twain also made a note of, "George and the stewed plums..." George Gillis was brother to Jim and Steve. Another note mentions, "J's [Jim's] Plums & Garlic." These are references to a story Twain told in his *Autobiography* about Jim Gillis eating the inedible fruit told in Chapter 2 of this book.

Mark Twain and Jim Gillis remained on Jackass Hill until January 22nd. Then they returned to Angel's Camp by way of Carson Hill. They apparently went to Angel's Camp to work

Angel's Hotel today, Angel's Camp, California, where Mark Twain first heard the story of the Jumping Frog. Author's photo.

Jim's pocket claim located in the nearby hills.

But their plans to prospect at Angel's Camp were fouled when two weeks of winter rains began on January 23rd. Twain and Gillis were forced to take a hotel room at Angel's Camp and broke up the monotony by going down to the "Frenchman's" for breakfast and dinner. The Frenchman's food was nothing to write home about. Twain wrote in his notebook, "beans & coffee only for breakfast & dinner every day at the French Restaurant at Angel's—bad, weak coffee—J[Jim] told waiter must made mistake—he asked for cafe—this was day-before-yesterday's dishwater..."

Trapped indoors while it rained, Twain made these notes in Notebook 4:

Jan. 23, 1865—Angels—Rainy, stormy—Beans and dishwater for breakfast at the Frenchman's, dishwater & beans for dinner, & both
articles warmed over for supper.
24th—Rained all day—meals as before
25—Same as above
26th—Rain, beans & dishwater—tapidaro [leather cover from a Mexican stirrup] *beef steak for a change—no use, could not bite it.*
27th—Same old diet—same old weather—went out to the "pocket"
claim—had to rush back.
28th—Rain & wind all day & all night.Chili beans & dishwater three times to-day, as usual, & some kind of "slum" which the Frenchman called "hash." Hash be d—d.
29th—The old, old thing. We shall have to stand the weather but as J [Jim] says, we won't stand this dishwater & beans any longer, by G—

Dinkelspiel store Vallecito, California where Mark Twain traded in January, 1865. Author's photo.

30th Jan.—Moved to the new hotel, just opened—good fare, & coffee that a Christian may drink without jeapordizing his eternal soul.

The "new hotel," or rather, their new lodgings, was likely Angels Hotel at the southern end of Angel's Camp. A canvass hotel in 1851, the tent was replaced by a one story wooden building, then by a stone building in 1855. In 1857, a second story was added. A saloon with a billiards table was located on the first floor on Main Street. The hotel stands today.

On the evening of January 25th, Mark Twain came very close to killing himself while taking a walk at Angel's Camp. He wrote in his notebook,

Narrow Escape__Jan 25 1865—Dark rainy night—walked to extreme edge of a cut in solid rock 30 feet deep—& while standing upon the extreme verge for a half dozen seconds, meditating whether to proceed or not, heard a stream of water falling into the cut, & then, my eyes becoming more accustomed to the darkness, saw that if the last step taken had been a hand breadth longer, must have plunged in. [One of Twain's feet projected over the edge as he stood.]

Around February 1st, Dick Stoker joined Twain and Gillis at Angel's Camp. February 3rd, Twain wrote in his notebook,

Dined at the Frenchman's, in order to let Dick see how he [the Frenchman] *does things. Had Hellfire soup & the old regular beans & dishwater. The Frenchman has 4 kinds of soup which he furnishes to customers only on great occasions. They are popularly known among the borders as Hellfire, General Debility, Insanity & Sudden Death, but it is not possible to describe them.*

The boys fooled around at the dinner table, "Talking like people 80 years old & toothless." [Notebook 4]

By February 6, two weeks of seasonal winter rains ended. The days now were warm with fair nights. For the next two weeks, Twain, Gillis and Stoker spent their days combing the hillsides near Angel's Camp for pocket mines. As usual, Twain sat under an oak tree and watched while Jim and Dick dug the ground and washed it in their pans. The boys camped beneath the oak trees spending their nights around the campfire and as Twain wrote in his notebook, "Camp meeting exhorting, slapping on back till make saddle boils." They were lazy, carefree days that

Mark Twain fondly looked back to the rest his life.

Roaming the Sierra foothills searching for gold and camping out reminded Twain of earlier prospecting trips he had made in Nevada and of other western experiences. During this time, he made several references in Notebook 4 of items he would later use in *Roughing It.*

For instance, around February 6, he wrote,"'Odd or Even'" —cast away at Honey Lake Smith's, " refers to the time Twain was stranded at Honey Lake Smith's east of Carson City while on a prospecting trip. Rains had caused the Carson River to swell to such a degree that the river could not be crossed safely. Twain and others were forced to stay in a crude hotel, "the whole place was crowded with teamsters, and we wore out every deck of cards in the place, and then had no amusement left but to scrape up a handful of vermin off the floor or the beds, and shuffle them, and bet odd or even," [Letter to *Territorial Enterprise*, February, 12, 1866. See also, "The Guests at "Honey Lake Smith's," Chapter 31, *Roughing It.*]

A following note refers to that same prospecting trip, "Billy Claggett moved fifteen steps from camp fire by the lice crawling on his back." Billy Claggett, Mark Twain, Gus Oliver and a Mr. Tillou made a trip to Unionville, a silver mining camp 200 miles northeast of Carson City in December, 1861. Twain turned the horrendous excursion into a very humorous episode in *Roughing It,* Chapters 26-30.

A third note refers to another story he included in *Roughing It.*

Bunker's great landslide case of Dick Sides vs. Rust— Rust's ranch slid down on Sides ranch & the suit was an ejectment suit tried before Gov Roop as Judge Referee, who gave a verdict in favor of the defendant.

Richard Sides was a Nevada rancher, landowner, and silver miner. Tom Rust was a Washoe Valley rancher. The above note refers to a story Twain told in Chapter 34 of *Roughing It*.

Slide Mountain is on the west side of Washoe Valley between Carson City and Reno, where the valley meets the steep Sierra Nevada. It is called Slide Mountain for a very good reason. Often, during spring snow melt, huge areas of snow, water, rock and dirt slide down the mountain. Only recently, a landslide washed out a number of houses, barns, etc. in the area. Yet, people still rebuild below the treacherous mountain.

In Mark Twain's story in *Roughing It*, Tom Morgan's ranch, located on Slide Mountain above Dick Hyde's, is moved on top of Hydes when a landslide carries Morgan's ranch, cabins and all, down the mountain. Hyde files suit and asks the judge to decide whose ranch it really is: Hydes or Morgan's.

In a last note Twain wrote, "Time Bob Howland came into Mrs. Murphy's corral in Carson, drunk, knocked down Wagners bottles of tarantulas & scorpions & spilled them on the floor." Bob Howland was a Carson City friend and roommate of Mark Twain's. The two prospected together at Aurora, Nevada. [See the author's, *Mark Twain: His Adventures At Aurora and Mono Lake*..] Twain transformed the above note into an hilarious account in "Escape of the Tarantulas," Chapter 21, *Roughing It*.

Like any good writer in search of material, Notebook 4 shows that Mark Twain was careful to make notes of useful incidents or stories he might later use. Sometimes he used the material many years later as in *Roughing It*, published in 1872, eight years after his visit to Jackass Hill and in *Huckleberry Finn*, published in 1885, twenty-one years later.

Around February 20th, the boys returned to Angel's Camp. At this time they once again visited the saloon at Angel's

Hotel. Here a dull bartender named Ben Coon, told Mark Twain a little story that would help change his life.

Twain made a simple, brief notation of the discovery in Notebook 4:

Coleman with his jumping frog—bet stranger $50—stranger had no frog, & C [Coleman] *got him one—in the meantime stranger filled C's* [Coleman's] *frog full of shot* [lead pellets] *& he couldn't jump—the stranger's frog won..*

Years later, Twain wrote a note in blue ink over this notation, "Wrote this story ["Jim Smiley and His Jumping Frog"] for Artemus [Ward]—his idiot publisher, Carleton gave it to [Henry] Clapp's *Saturday Press.*" Artemus Ward was one of the most popular humorists in America at this time. Twain and Ward had met a year earlier in Virginia City where Ward had performed his stand-up show, "Babes In The Wood," the format of which Twain later incorporated into his own popular lectures. Twain and Ward became friends during Ward's brief visit.

About the time Twain was living on Jackass Hill, Ward remembered Twain's humor and wrote him asking him to submit a story for his upcoming book, *Artemus Ward; His Travels.* Twain would eventually submit the "Jumping Frog," to Ward's publisher which would arrive too late. Ward's publisher would pass the "Jumping Frog," on to another publisher.

In March 18, 1865, in "An Unbiased Criticism," published in the *Californian*, Twain wrote that the person who first told him the "Jumping Frog" story was an ex-corporal [Ben] Coon, "a nice baldheaded man at Angel's Camp." Twain later depicted the narrator of the "Jumping Frog," as:

...a dull person, and ignorant; he had no gift as a story-teller, and

no invention; in his mouth this episode was merely history—history and statistics; and the gravest sort of history, too, he was entirely serious, for he was dealing with what to him were austere facts, and they interested him solely because they were facts; he was drawing on his memory, not his mind; he saw no humor in his tale, neither did his listeners; neither he nor they ever smiled or laughed,...

Private History of the 'Jumping Frog' Story," North American Review, April, 1894

Dull or not, Ben Coon presented Mark Twain with the idea for a short story that would do more for his career and fame, than all the articles he had written in the past two years.

Robinson's Ferry on the Stanislaus River where Mark Twain and Jim Gillis crossed the river on their way back to Jackass Hill from Angel's Camp. The site is now beneath the water of the New Melones dam. Photo courtesy of the Tuolumne County Historical Society.

Chapter 4

Jim Smiley and His Jumping Frog

February 20th, 1865, Mark Twain left Angel's Camp and returned to Jackass Hill with Jim Gillis and Dick Stoker. Two days later, he borrowed a horse and rode to Copperopolis, 12 miles west of Angel's Camp, where he stayed for two days. February 25th, he left Copperopolis by stage for San Francisco by way of Stockton.

Arriving in San Francisco, Twain took a room at his old haunt, the Occidental Hotel. There he picked up his mail, some of which had been there for several months. Among the mail was a letter from Artemus Ward, which requested that Twain submit a story for Ward's upcoming book.

For unknown reasons, Twain did not immediately respond to Ward's request. Eight months later, in October, 1865, Twain mailed Ward his version of the story he first heard at Angel's Camp, "Jim Smiley and His Jumping Frog." Ward received the story October 18, 1865, too late for publication in his book. Ward's publisher, without the consent of Mark Twain, passed the story on to Henry Clapp, editor of the New York *Saturday Press.*. Clapp published the "Jumping Frog," in the *Saturday Press*, November 18, 1865.

Like many incidents in Mark Twain's life, the publication of the "Jumping Frog," in the *Saturday Press*, proved remarkably fortunate. As was the common custom of the time, the story was copied and reprinted by numerous newspapers throughout America and Europe. This caused the "Jumping Frog " to reach a greater audience than if it had been published in Artemus Ward's book, which ironically, died a quick, silent death.

Here then, is Mark Twain's version of the story he first heard in the worn-out saloon at Angel's Camp, with his miner friends, Jim Gillis and Dick Stoker:

In compliance with the request of a friend of mine, who wrote me from the East, I called on good-natured, garrulous old Simon Wheeler, and inquired after my friend's friend, *Leonidas W.* Smiley, as requested to do, and I hereunto append the result. I have a lurking suspicion that Leonidas W. Smiley is a myth; that my friend never knew such a personage; and that he only conjectured that if I asked old Wheeler about him, it would remind him of his infamous *Jim* Smiley, and he would go to work and bore me to death with some exasperating reminiscence of him as long and as tedious as it should be useless to me. If that was the design, it succeeded.

I found Simon Wheeler dozing comfortably by the bar-room stove of the dilapidated tavern in the decayed mining camp of Angel's, and I noticed that he was fat and bald-headed, and had an expression of winning gentleness and simplicity upon his tranquil countenance. He roused up, and gave me good day. I told him that a friend of mine had commissioned me to make some inquiries about a cherished companion of his boyhood named *Leonidas W*. Smiley—*Rev. Leonidas W*. Smiley, a young minister of the Gospel, who he had heard was at one time a resident of Angel's Camp. I added that if Mr. Wheeler could tell me anything about this Rev. Leonidas W. Smiley, I would feel under many obligations to him.

Simon Wheeler backed me into a corner and blockaded me there with his chair, and then sat down and reeled off the monotonous narrative which follows this paragraph. He never smiled, he never frowned, he never changed his voice from the gentle flowing key to which he turned his initial sentence, he never betrayed the slightest suspicion of enthusiasm; but all through the interminable narrative there ran a vein of impressive earnestness and sincerity, which showed me plainly that, so far from his imagining that there was anything ridiculous or funny about his story, he regarded it as a really important matter, and admired its two heros as men of transcendent genius in finess. I let him go on his own way, and never interrupted him once.

''Rev. Leonidas W. H'm, Reverend Le—well, there was a feller here once by the name of Jim Smiley, in the winter of ' 49—or maybe it was the spring of ' 50—I don't recollect exactly, somehow, though what makes me think it was one or the other is because I remember the big flume warn't finished when he first come to the camp; but anyway, he was the curiousest man about always betting on anything that turned up you ever see, if he could get anybody to bet on the other side; and if he couldn't he'd change sides. Any way that suited the other man would suit *him*— any way just so's he got a bet, *he* was satisfied. But still he was lucky, uncommon lucky; he most always come out winner. He was always ready and laying for a chance; there couldn't be no solit'ry thing mentioned but that feller'd offer to bet on it, and take ary side you please, as I was just telling you. If there was a horse-race, you'd find him flush or you'd find him busted at the end of it; if there was a dog-fight, he'd bet on it; if there was a cat-fight, he'd bet on it; if there was a chicken-fight, he'd bet on it; why, if there was two birds setting on a fence, he would bet you which one would fly first; or if there was a camp-meeting, he would be there reg'lar to bet on Parson Walker, which he judged to be the best exhorter about here, and so he was too, and a good man. If he even see a straddle-bug start to anywheres, he would bet you how long it would take him to get to—to wherever he was going to, and if you took him up, he would foller that straddle-bug to Mexico but what he would find out where he was bound for and how long he was on the road. Lots of the boys here has seen that Smiley, and can tell you about him. Why, it never made no difference to *him*—he'd bet on any thing—the dangdest feller. Parson Walker's wife laid very sick once, for a good while, and it seemed as if they warn't going to save her; but one morning he come in, and Smiley up and asked him how she was, and he said she was considerable better-thank the Lord for his inf'nite mercy—and coming on so smart that with the blessing of Prov'dence she'd get wll yet; and Smiley, before he thought, says, ' Well, I'll resk two-and-a-half she don't anyway.'

"Thish-yer Smiley had a mare—the boys called her the fifteen-minute nag, but that was only in fun, you know, because of course she was faster than that—and he used to win money on that horse, for all she was so slow and always had the asthma, or the distemper, or the consumption, or something of that kind. They used to give her two or three hundred yards' start, and then pass her under way; but always at the fag end of the race she'd get excited and desperate like, and come convorting and straddling up, and scattering her legs around limber, sometimes in the air, and sometimes out to one side among the fences, and kicking up m-o-r-e racket with her coughing and sneezing and blowing her nose—and always fetch up at the stand just about a neck ahead, as near as you could cipher it down.

" And he had a little small bull-pup, that to look at him you'd think he warn't worth a cent but to set around and look ornery and lay for a chance to steal something. But as soon as money was up on him he was a different dog; his under-jaw'd begin to stick out like the fo'castle of a steamboat, and his teeth would uncover and shine like the furnaces. And a dog might tackle him and bully-rag him, and bite him, and throw him over his shoulder two or three times, and Andrew Jackson—which was the name of the pup—Andrew Jackson would never let on but what *he* was satisfied, and hadn't expected nothing else and the bets being doubled and doubled on the other side all the time, till the money was all up; and then all of a sudden he would grab that other dog jest by the j'int of his hind leg and freeze to it—not chaw, you understand, but only just grip and hang on till they throwed up the sponge, if it was a year. Smiley always come out winner on that pup, till he harnessed a dog once that didn't have no hind legs, because they'd been sawed off in a circular saw, and when the thing had gone along far enough, and the money was all up, and he come to make a snatch for his pet holt, he see in a minute how he'd been imposed on, and how the other dog had him in the door, so to speak, and he 'peared surprised, and then he looked sorter discouraged-like, and didn't try no more to win the fight, and so he got shucked out bad. He give Smiley a look, as much as to say his heart was broke, and it was *his* fault, for putting up a dog that hadn't no hind legs for him to take holt of, which was his main dependence in a fight, and then he limped off a piece and laid down and died. It was a good pup, was that Andrew Jackson, and would have made a name for hisself if he'd lived, for the stuff was in him and he had genius—I know it, because he hadn't no opportunities to speak of, and it don't stand to reason that a dog could make such a fight as he could under them circumstances if he hadn't no talent. It always makes me feel sorry when I think of that last fight of his'n, and the way it turned out.

"Well, Thish-yer Smiley had rat-tarriers, and chicken cocks, and tomcats and all them kind of things, till you couldn't rest, and you couldn't fetch nothing for him to bet on but he'd match you. He ketched a frog one day, and took him home, and said he cal'lated to educate him; and so he never done nothing for three months but set in his back yard and learn that frog to jump. And you bet you he did learn him, too. He'd give him a little punch behind, and the next minute you'd see that frog whirling in the air like a doughnut—see him turn one summerset, or maybe a couple, if he got a good start, and come down flat-footed and all right, like a cat. He got him up so in the matter of ketching flies, and kep' him in practice so constant, that he'd nail a fly every time as fur as he could see him. Smiley said all a frog wanted was education, and he could do 'most anything—and I believe him. Why, I've seen him set Dan'l Webster down on this floor—Dan'l Webster was the name of the frog-and sing out, "Flies, Dan'l, flies!' and quicker'n you could wink he'd spring straight up and snake a fly off'n the counter there, and flop down on the floor ag'in as solid as a gob of mud, and fall to scratching the side of his head with his hind foot as indifferent as if he hadn't no idea he'd been doin' any more'n any frog might do. You never see a frog so modest andstraight-for'ard as he was, for all he was so gifted. And when it come to fair and square jumping on a dead level, he could get over more ground at one straddle than any animal of his breed you ever see. Jumping on dead level was his strong suit, you understand; and when it come to that, Smiley would ante up money on him as long as he had a red. Smiley was monstrous proud of his frog, and well he might be, for fellers that had traveled and been everywheres all said he laid over any frog that ever they see.

"Well, Smiley kep' the beast in a little lattice box, and he used to fetch him down-town sometimes and lay for a bet. One day a feller-a stranger in the camp, he was-come acrost him with his box, and says:

"What might it be that you've got in the box?"

"And Smiley says, sorter indifferent-like, 'It might be a parrot, or it might be a canary, maybe, but it ain't-it's only just a frog.'

"And the feller took it, and looked at it careful, and turned it round this way and that, and says, 'H'm-so 'tis. Well, what's he good for?

"'Well,' Smiley says, easy and careless, 'he's good enough for one thing, I should judge—he can outjump any frog in Calaveras County.'

"The feller took the box again, and took another long, particular look, and give it back to Smiley, and says, very deliberate, 'Well,' he says, ' I don't see no p'ints about that frog that's any better'n any other frog.'

"'Maybe you don't,' Smiley says. 'Maybe you understand frogs and maybe you don't understand 'em; maybe you've had experience, and maybeyou ain't only a amature, as it were. Anyways, I've got my opinion, and I'll resk forty dollars that he can outjump any frog in Calaveras County.'

"And the feller studied a minute, and then says, kinder sad-like, 'Well, I'm only a stranger here, and I ain't got no frog; but if I had a frog, I'd bet you.'

"And then Smiley says, 'That's all right—that's all right—if you'll hold my box a minute, I'll go and get you a frog.' And so the feller took the box, and put up his forty dollars along with Smiley's, and set down to wait.

"So he set there a good while thinking and thinking to himself, and then he got the frog out and prized his mouth open and took a teaspoon and filled him full of quail-shot-filled him pretty near up to his chin-and set him on the floor. Smiley he went to the swamp and slopped around in the mud for a long time, and finally he ketched a frog, and fetched him in, and give him to this feller, and says:

"'' Now, if you're ready, set him alongside on Dan'l, with his fore paws just even with Dan'l's, and I'll give the word.' Then he says, 'One—two—three—git!' and him and the feller touched up the frogs from behind, and the new frog hopped off lively, but Dan'l give a heave, and hysted up his shoulders—so—like a Frenchman, but it warn't no use—he couldn't budge; he was planted as solid as a church, and he couldn't no more stir than if he was anchored out. Smiley was a good deal surprised, and he was disgusted too, but he didn't have no idea what the matter was, of course.

"The feller took the money and started away; and when he was going out the door, he sorter jerked his thumb over his shoulder—so—at Dan'l and says again, very deliberate, 'Well,'he says, '*I* don't see no p'ints about that frog that's any better'n any other frog.'

"Smiley he stood scratching his head and looking down at Dan'l a Long time, and last he says, 'I do wonder what in the nation that frog throw'd off for—I wonder if there ain't something the matter with him—he 'pears to look mighty baggy, somehow.' And he ketched Dan'l by the nap of the neck, and hefted him, and says, 'Why blame my cats if he don't weigh five pound!' and turned him upside down and he belched out a double handful of shot. And then he see how it was, and he was the maddest man-he set the frog down and took out after that feller, but he never ketched him. And—"

Here Simon Wheeler heard his name called from the front yard, and got up to see what was wanted. And turning to me as he moved away, he said: "Just set where you are, stranger, and rest easy—I ain't going to be gone a second."

But, by your leave, I did not think that a continuation of the history of the enterprising vagabond *Jim* Smiley would be likely to afford me much information concerning the *Rev. Leonidas W.* Smiley, and so I started away.

At the door I met the sociable Wheeler returning, and he buttonholed me and recommenced:

"Well, thish-yer Smiley had a yaller one-eyed cow that didn't have no tail, only just a short stump like a bannanner, and—"

However, lacking both time and inclination, I did not wait to hear about the afflicted cow, but took my leave.

Two hotels in Copperopolis where Mark Twain may have
stayed in February, 1865. Author's photo.

Epilogue

When Mark Twain returned to San Francisco in late February, 1865, he continued contributing articles for the *Californian*, at $12 each. By mid-June he was writing daily correspondent letters for the *Enterprise* from which he earned $100 a month.

Twain's *Californian* writings managed to attract attention in the East when the New York *Round Table* acknowledged Twain as a humorist on the rise. October 18, 1865, the San Francisco *Dramatic Chronicle* [today's *San Francisco Chronicle*] reprinted the *Round Table's* comments in a clip, "Recognized." The editor of the *Round Table* wrote:

The foremost among the merry gentlemen of the California press, as far as we have been able to judge, is one who signs himself "Mark Twain." Of his real name we are ignorant, but his style resembles that of "John Phoenix" more nearly than any other, and some things we have seen from his pen would do honor to the memory of even that chieftain among humorists. He is, we believe, quite a young man, and has not written a great deal. Perhaps, if he will husband his resources and not kill with overwork the mental goose that has given us these golden eggs, he may one day take rank among the brightest of our wits.

"American Humor and Humorists," Round Table, Sept 9, 1865

Twain was encouraged by the *Round Table's* attention and wrote his brother about the notice:

...I have had a "call" to literature, of a low order—i.e. humorous. It is nothing to be proud of, but it is my strongest suit, & if I were to listen to that maxim of stern duty which says that to do right you must multiply the one or the two or the three talents which the Almighty entrusts to your keeping, I would long ago have ceased to meddle with things for which I was by nature unfitted & turned my attention to seriously scribbling to excite the laughter of God's creatures. Poor, pitiful business! Though the Almighty did His part by me—for the talent is a mighty engine when supplied with the steam of education,—which I have not got, & so its pistons & cylinders & shafts move feebly & for a holiday show & are useless for any good purpose...You see in me a talent for humorous writing, & urge me to cultivate it...now, when editors of standard literary papers in the distant east give me high praise, & who do not know me & cannot of course be blinded by the glamour of partiality, that I really begin to believe there must be something in it...I will drop all trifling, & sighing after vain impossibilities, & strive for a fame—unworthy & evanescent though it must of necessity be—if you will record your promise to go hence to the States & preach the gospel when circumstances shall enable you to do so? I am in earnest. Shall it be so?

Letter to Orion and Mollie Clemens, Oct. 19 and 20, 1865

Though earning a fair living as a full time writer, Twain admitted in the same letter that he was still in debt.

When "Jim Smiley and His Jumping Frog," was published November 18, 1865 in the New York *Saturday Press*, it received attention and high praises in New York. The San Francisco *Alta California* noted the tale's success when its New York correspondent, Richard L. Ogden wrote,

Mark Twain's story in the Saturday Press of November 18, called "Jim Smiley and His Jumping Frog," has set all New York in a roar. I have been asked fifty times about it and its author, and the papers are copying it far and near. It is voted the best thing of the day. Cannot the Californian *afford to keep Mark all to itself? It should not let him scintilate so widely without first being filtered through the California press.*

Despite the "Jumping Frog's" success, Twain was somewhat disturbed by it. He wrote his mother and sister:

...To think that after writing many an article a man might be excused for thinking tolerably good, those New York people should single out a villainous backwoods sketch to compliment me on!—"Jim Smiley and His Jumping Frog"—a squib which would never have been written but to please Artemus Ward, & then it reached New York too late to appear in his book. [*Artemus Ward; His Travels*]

Letter to Jane Lampton Clemens and Pamela Moffett, January 20, 1866

On March 7, 1866, Mark Twain sailed from San Francisco aboard the *Ajax* to the Sandwich (Hawaiian) Islands as a special correspondent for the Sacramento *Union*. He intended to stay on the Islands a month, but stayed five months. During this time he gathered material for twenty-five correspondent letters, most of which he wrote while on the Islands. Twain intended to publish these letters as a book about the Sandwich Islands. The Sandwich Island letters eventually provided the basis for chapters 62-77 of *Roughing It*.

By August 13, 1866, Twain was back in San Francisco. During the last half of the month, he completed the remainder of his Sandwich Island letters for the *Union*. He also began submitting articles for the New York *Weekly Review*. Again in September, the *Union* hired Twain to cover the California State Agricultural Society at Sacramento.

October 2, encouraged by friends, Twain gave his second humorous lecture on the Sandwich Islands at Maguire's Academy of Music in San Francisco. [His first lecture was given in Carson City, January 27, 1863, as a benefit for the First Presbyterian Church.] The lecture was a great success and led to a quick tour of several California and Nevada mining towns, including Virginia City, where Twain lectured on October 31. Piper's Opera House was crammed. Twain's hour and a half lecture brought the house down.

December 15, 1866, Mark Twain sailed from San Francisco for New York. He had been hired by the San Francisco *Alta California* as a travelling correspondent. The *Alta* wrote,

"Mark Twain" goes off on his journey over the world as the Travelling Correspondent of the ALTA CALIFORNIA, not stinted as to time, place or direction—writing his weekly letter on such subjects and from such places as will best suit him; but we

may say that he will first visit the home of his youth—St. Louis— thence through the principal cities to the Atlantic seaboard again, crossing the ocean to visit the "Universal Exposition" at Paris, through Italy, the Mediterranean, India, China, Japan, and back to San Francisco by the China Mail Steamship line. That his letters will be read with interest needs no assurance from us—his reputation has been made here in California, and his great ability is well known; but he has been known principally as a humorist, while he really has no superior as a descriptive writer—a keen observer of men and their surroundings—and we feel confident his letters to the ALTA, from his new field of observation will give him world-wide reputation.

"Mark Twain's Farewell, " Alta California, December 15, 1866

Twain eventually sailed from New York, June 8, 1867, aboard the *Quaker City* for the Holy Land. During this trip, Twain wrote a series of travel letters for the *Alta California* .

When Twain returned to America in November, 1867, he settled in Washington, D.C. at Nevada Senator William Stewart's house where he began writing *The Innocents Abroad*, based on the *Quaker City* letters. During the ensuing months a dispute arose between Twain and the *Alta California* regarding Twain's use of the letters in his book. In order to secure their rights, Twain sailed to California in March, 1868. There he persuaded the *Alta's* publishers to allow him to use the letters.

In April, Twain gave lectures on his travels to the Holy Land in San Francisco and in Virginia City, April 24.

Through the spring and early summer, Twain continued writing his first draft of *The Innocents Abroad*, in San Francisco.

On July 6, 1868, Mark Twain sailed from San Francisco

for New York. This time he was leaving California for good.

Twain's years in Nevada and California, led to the writing and publication of his first two books: *The Innocents Abroad*, published in 1869, was a literary and financial success followed in 1872 by, *Roughing It*, a well written hilarious account of Twain's experiences in the Far West. Included in *Roughing It*, were many of those Twain had known in the West, including Jim Gillis and Dick Stoker.

Before leaving for the Sandwich Islands, Twain had written Billy Gillis to apologize for losing his temper one evening on Jackass Hill. Twain told Billy,

As in the course of human events we may not meet again, I will unburden my conscience of a load it has been carrying ever since the night of the serenade you and your band of troubadors attempted to give me. When you came into the cabin after I had scared the other boys off the hill, I was in a mighty ugly mood and I just wanted the chance you gave me to vent my spleen on somebody or something. I called you some pretty hard names, which I knew at the time were undeserved, and accused you of high crimes and misdemeanors of which I knew you were not guilty. I wanted to ask your pardon the next morning when you called me to breakfast, but courage failed me and I put off doing so to a more "convenient season." That season has now arrived, and I do ask you to forgive me. Tell the boys that I am often with them in my dreams, and that when I return to the city I will come back to them once more on Old Jackass, if I can possibly arrange to do so.

Letter to William R. Gillis , 3? March, 1866

Mark Twain did not make it back to Jackass Hill and he

never saw the Gillises again after he left California. Occasionally they corresponded over the many years they were apart.

About two weeks before Mark Twain married Olivia Langdon, he wrote Jim Gillis on Jackass Hill:

...It makes my heart ache yet to call to mind some of those days. Still, it shouldn't—for right in the depths of their poverty and their pocket hunting vagabondage lay the germ of my coming good fortune. You remember the one gleam of jollity, that shot across our dismal sojourn in the rain and mud of Angel's Camp—I mean that day we sat around the tavern stove and heard that chap tell about the frog and how they filled him with shot. And you remember how we quoted from the yarn and laughed over it, out there on the hillside while you and dear old Stoker panned and washed. I jotted down the story in my notebook that day and I would have been glad to get ten or fifteen dollars for it—I was just that blind. I published that story, and it became widely known in America, India, China, England—and the reputation it made for me has paid me thousands and thousands of dollars since.

...wouldn't I love to take old Stoker by the hand and wouldn't I love to see him in his great specialty, his wonderful rendition of "Rinaldo" in the "Burning Shame!" Where is Dick and what is he doing? Give him my fervent love and warm old remembrances.

A week from today I shall be married to a girl even better than Mahala, and lovelier than the peerless "Chaparral Quails." You can't come so far, Jim, but still I cordially invite you to come, anyhow—and I invite Dick, too. And if you two boys were to land here on that pleasant occasion, we would make you right royally welcome...

Remember me to the boys—and recollect, Jim, that whenever you or Dick shall chance to stumble into Buffalo, we shall have a knife and fork for you and an honest welcome.

Truly Your Friend

Saml L. Clemens

    P.S. California plums are good, Jim, particularly when they are stewed.
    Do they continue to name all the young Injuns after me—when you pay them for a compliment?

Letter to Jim Gillis, January 20, 1870

    "Jim Smiley and His Jumping Frog," was re-published in 1867 in a collection of Twain's Western writings as, *The Celebrated Jumping Frog of Calaveras County, and Other Sketches.* [Some consider this Mark Twain's first book. I consider it a collection of early sketches. *The Innocents Abroad* was Mark Twain's first deliberate book.] The "Jumping Frog" grew in popularity and became known as both "The Celebrated Jumping Frog of Calaveras County, " and "The Notorious Jumping Frog of Calaveras County." For years Twain was noted in America and abroad as the author of the "Jumping Frog," the story that did more for his first worldwide recognition than anything else.
    Though Mark Twain often spoke and wrote of returning to California, he never did. For the next forty-six years of Mark Twain's life, Jackass Hill glowed warmly in his memory as a "sylvan paradise," forever a part of his adventurous, free-wheeling youth.

Jackass Hill Chronology

May 29, 1864: Mark Twain leaves Virginia City with Steve Gillis for San Francisco.

June: Moves into Occidental Hotel in San Francisco.

June 6: Begins reporting for San Francisco *Call*.

July: Mark and Steve Gillis move into new lodgings, address unknown.Begins submitting articles for the *Califor nian*.

September 17: Writes Dan De Quille and asks him to buy his furniture. Looking for ways to earn money. Quits working nights for the *Call*.

September 28: Writes his older brother, Orion, and asks that his "files," be sent to him, in preparation for writing his first book.

Mid-October: Quits reporting for the *Call*. Concentrates on writing articles for the *Californian* , a West Coast literary journal, for which he is paid $12 each.

Late November: Steve Gillis nearly kills a man in barroom brawl. Mark Twain posts Gillis' bond.

Early December: Mark Twain leaves for Jim Gillis's cabin on Jackass Hill near Sonora. Stays on Jackass Hill through Christmas. Much time is spent telling each other anecdotes and humorous stories.

New Year's, 1865: Spent at Vallecito, Calaveras County, not far from Jackass Hill.

January 3rd: Returns to Jackass Hill with Jim Gillis by way of Angel's Camp and Robinson's Ferry across the Stanislaus River.

January 22nd: At Angel's Camp

January 25th: Twain nearly kills himself at Angel's Camp by falling into a canyon at night. About this time meets

Ben Coon at Angel's Hotel,   who tells Twain the story of the Jumping Frog.

January 30th: Stays at Angel's Hotel.

February 6: Rain ends. Days are warm and sunny. Begins prospecting around Angel's Camp with Jim Gillis and Dick Stoker.

February 20th: Leaves Angel's Camp for Jackass Hill with Jim Gillis and Dick Stoker in a snow storm.

February 21st: On Jackass Hill again.

February 23rd: Leaves Jackass Hill by horse for Copperopolis.

February 25th: Leaves Copperopolis by stage for San Francisco via Stockton.

February 26th: Home again at the Occidental Hotel in San Francisco. Receives letter from Artemus Ward requesting a story for his upcoming book.

October: Submits "Jim Smiley and His Jumping Frog," for Ward's book. Story arrives in New York too late for publication.

November 18, 1865: "Jim Smiley and His Jumping Frog," sent by Ward's publisher to the editor of New York *Saturday Press*, is published. Story becomes immensely popular and is re-printed by newspapers throughout America and Europe. "Jumping Frog," earns Twain his first national notoriety.

March 7, 1866: Sails to the Sandwich Islands as a correspondent for the Sacramento *Union*.

June 25: Writes dispatch about the burning of the clipper ship, *Hornet*, and its survivors. *Hornet* articles help cement Twain's West Coast career.

October 2: Gives his second humorous lecture on the Sandwich Islands in at Maguire's Academy of Music, San

Francisco.

December 15: Leaves California for New York by ship.

June 8, 1867: Sails from New York aboard the *Quaker City* for the Holy Land as a correspondent for the San Francisco *Alta California*.

November 19: Returns to New York. Moves to Washington, D.C. where he begins writing *The Innocents Abroad*, based on letters written for the *Alta California*.

March, 1868: Returns to California in order to secure rights to *Quaker City* letters.

April-June: Continues writing first draft of *The Innocents Abroad*.

July 6, 1868: Leaves California for good.

1869: *The Innocents Abroad* is published; becomes an immediate success.

1872: *Roughing It*, published, another success.

Acknowledgements

As always, I would like to thank my wife, Edie, for her encouragement and love. Edie read and re-read the manuscript, caught many errors and made suggestions which improved the manuscript.

Again, the staff of the Mark Twain Project, University of California Berkeley, was a big help, supplying the author with copies of Twain's original letters and with photographs.

My thanks to the Tuolumne Historical Society and Museum for supplying several photographs published in this book.

I owe a big thanks to the many researchers and authors who have written many enlightening books on Twain's life and writings, some of which appear in the bibliography. Authors who deserve special mention are: Albert Bigelow Paine, Effie Monna Mack, Paul Fatout, Henry Nash Smith, Ivan Benson and Justin Kaplan.

As always, I am eternally in debt to my Lord, Jesus Christ, who has endured me through my long journey to Him. I thank you Lord for your patience, for your love, your mercy, your salvation. And I thank you for the abilities you have given me which help me to research and write books, here on Your earth.

Selected Bibliography

Unpublished Sources:

The Mark Twain Papers, Mark Twain Project, University of California, Berkeley

William Wright Correspondence, Bancroft Library, University of California, Berkeley

Newspaper and Magazine Sources:

Territorial Enterprise
Gold Hill News
Golden Era
The Californian
Virginia Daily Union
Virginia Evening Bulletin
Virginia Chronicle
San Francisco Call
San Francisco Bulletin
OLD PIUTE
Alta California
Sacramento Union
California Illustrated Magazine
Nevada Magazine
North American Review

Books and Articles:

Barnes, George E. "Mark Twain. As He Was Known During His Stay on the Pacific Slope," San Francisco *Morning Call*, April 17, 1887, page 1.

Benson, Ivan: *Mark Twain's Western Years*, Russell and Russell, 1938.

Branch, Edgar Marquess: *The Literary Apprenticeship of Mark Twain*, University of Illinois Press, 1958; *Clemens of the "Call", Mark Twain In San Francisco,* University of California Press, 1969.

Browne, Lena F.: *J. Ross Browne: His Letters, Journals and Writing*, University of New Mexico Press, 1969.

Clemens, Clara: *My Father Mark Twain*, Harper and Bros., 1931.

Clemens, Susy: *Papa An Intimate Biography of Mark Twain*, edited and an introduction by Charles Neider, Doubleday & Company, Inc., Garden City, New York, 1985.

Day, A. Grove: editor, *Mark Twain's Letters From Hawaii*, University Press of Hawaii, 1966.

De Quille, Dan: *The Big Bonanza*, Alfred Knopf, 1947, *"Reporting With Mark Twain,"* California Illustrated Magazine, Vol. IV, 1893; *"Artemus Ward In Nevada, "* California Illustrated Magazine, August, 1893.

DeVoto, Bernard: *Mark Twain's America*, Houghton Mifflin Company, 1932.

Doten, Alfred: *The Journals of Alfred Doten*, edited by Walter Van Tilburg Clark, University of Nevada Press, 1973. *"Early Journalism in Nevada*, The Nevada Magazine, Vol. I, No. 3, 1899.

Fatout, Paul: *Mark Twain In Virginia City*, Indiana University Press, 1964.

Frady, Steven R.: *Red Shirts and Leather Helmets*, University of Nevada Press, 1984.

Gillis, William: *Memories of Mark Twain and Steve Gillis*, The Banner, 1924.

Goodwin, Charles C.: *As I Remember Them*, Salt Lake Commercial Club, 1913.

Howells, W.D.: *My Mark Twain*, Harper and Bros., 1911.

Kaplan, Justin: *Mr Clemens and Mark Twain*, Simon and Schuster, New

York, 1966.

Kelly, J. Wells: *First Directory of Nevada Territory*, San Francisco, 1862. *Second Directory of Nevada Territory*, 1863.

Lewis, Oscar: *Silver Kings*, Alfred Knopf, 1947.

Long, E. Hudson: *Mark Twain Handbook*, Hendricks House, 1957.

Mack, Effie Mona: *Mark Twain In Nevada*, Charles Scribner's Sons, 1947.

Moody, Eric: *Western Carpetbagger*, University of Nevada Press, 1978.

Paine, Albert Bigelow: *Mark Twain: A Biography*, Harper and Bros., 1912. *Mark Twain's Letters, Vol. I*, Harper and Bros., 1917.

Rogers, Franklin: *The Pattern For Mark Twain's Roughing It*, University of California Press, 1961.

Smith, Henry Nash and Frederick Anderson: *Mark Twain Of The Enterprise*, University of California Press, 1957.

Stewart, William M.: *Reminiscences*, Neale Publishing Co., 1908.

Twain, Mark: *The Autobiography of Mark Twain*, edited by Charles Neider, Harper and Row, 1959; "Curing A Cold, " "My Bloody Massacre," "My Late Senatorial Secretaryship;" *Huckleberry Finn*; *Life On The Mississippi*; *Roughing It*;*,Sketches New and Old*;*The Innocents Abroad, Tom Sawyer;* personal letters 1864 and 1865;""Private History of the 'Jumping Frog' Story," North American Review, April, 1894; *Mark Twain's Letters, Volume 1, 1853-1866*, Edited by Edgar Marquess Branch, Michael B. Frank and Kenneth M. Sanderson, University of California Press, 1988; Notebook 4; *The Complete Humorous Sketches and Tales of Mark Twain*, edited by Charles Neider, Hanover House, Garden City, NY, 1961; *A Pen Warmed Up in Hell, Mark Twain In Protest*, edited by Frederick Anderson, Harper and Row, 1972.

Weisenberger, Francis Phelps: *Idol of The West*, Syracuse University

Press, 1965.

Index

List of Illustrations

Order these great books by mail today
Autographed and inscribed by George Williams III.
Or use our web site to order:
www.autographed-books.com

IN THE LAST OF THE WILD WEST. True story of the author's efforts to expose the murders of brothel prostitutes in Storey County, Nevada, home of the largest legal brothel in the world. 256 pages. $12.95.

ROSA MAY: THE SEARCH FOR A MINING CAMP LEGEND Virginia city, Carson City and Bodie, California were towns Rosa May worked as a prostitute and madam 1873-1912. Read her remarkable true story based on 3 1/2 years of research. Praised by the *Los Angeles Times*. Includes 30 rare photos, 26 personal letters. 240 pages. $11.95.

THE REDLIGHT LADIES OF VIRGINIA CITY, NEVADA In the 1870's Virginia City had the largest redlight district in America. Here are the true stories of the women who plied their trade. 48 pages. $6.95.

THE GUIDE TO BODIE AND EASTERN SIERRA HISTORIC SITES True story of the rise and fall of Bodie, California's most famous mining camp, today a ghost town, National Historic Site and California State Park. Guide maps and 100 photos on an 8 1/2 X 11 format. 88 pages. $12.95.

HOT SPRINGS OF THE EASTERN SIERRA Here are more than 40 hot springs in the Eastern Sierra, many secret springs only known to locals. Maps by the author help you find these secret springs easily. $10.95.

New! HOT SPRINGS OF NORTHERN CALIFORNIA. Here are more than 45 recreational hot springs from as far south as Bishop, California north to the Oregon border. $12.95

New! HOT SPRINGS OF NEVADA . Includes every recreational hot spring in Nevada. There are some wonderful places here. Most of the hot springs are on public lands and they are free to use. $10.95

THE MURDERS AT CONVICT LAKE True story of the infamous 1871 Nevada State Penitentiary break in which 29 outlaws escaped and fled more than 250 miles into Mono and Inyo counties, California. They vowed to kill anyone who got in their way. In a terrible shootout at Monte Diablo, today known as Convict Lake just south of Mammoth Lakes ski resort, the convicts killed two men. $5.95 .

MARK TWAIN: HIS ADVENTURES AT AURORA AND MONO LAKE
When Sam Clemens arrived in Nevada in 1861, he wanted to get rich quick. He tried silver mining at Aurora, Nevada near Mono Lake not far from Yosemite National Park. Clemens didn't strike it rich but his hard luck mining days led to his literary career. 32 rare photos, mining deeds and maps to places where Clemens lived, wrote and camped. 100 pages. $8.95

NEW! MARK TWAIN: HIS LIFE IN VIRGINIA CITY, NEVADA While reporting for the *Territorial Enterprise* in Virginia City, 1862-64, Sam Clemens adopted his well known pen name, Mark Twain. Here is the lively account of Mark Twain's early writing days in the most exciting town in the West. 60 rare photos and maps to places Twain lived and wrote. 208 pages. $10.95

Mark Twain and the Jumping Frog of Calaveras County . Mark Twain's Jumping Frog story launched his international career. After getting run out of Virginia City, Twain settled in San Francisco in May, 1864. After a discouraging prospecting trip, in a saloon at Angel's Camp, Twain was told the Jumping Frog story by a bartender. Twain's version, published eleven months later, became an international hit. "The Celebrated Jumping Frog of Calaveras County," is included in this book. 116 pages, index, bibliography, 35 historic photographs, guide maps for travelers. $ 8.95

New! Special Golden Embossed and Numbered Hard Cover Edition
ON THE ROAD WITH MARK TWAIN IN CALIFORNIA AND NEVADA
Praised by the national *Library Journal* and the San Francisco *Chronicle*. Here is a handy, easy to read guide to Mark Twain's haunts in California and Nevada 1861-68. Has road directions to historic sites, guide maps and more than 100 photographs of Twain, the historic sites and Twain's friends. Gives brief run-downs of each place and tells what Twain was doing while there. A must-have book for any Twain fan who would like to follow his trail in the far West. 136 pages, road maps, index. $29.95

New! Updated Edition of one of the most important books on today's Music Business
THE SONGWRITER'S DEMO MANUAL AND SUCCESS GUIDE shows the songwriter and aspiring group how to make a professional demo tape at home or in the studio and how to use it to sell songs and land record deals. The author explains how the music business operates, who the important people are and how to make contact with them. 8 1/2x11 format in a ring binder 125 pages with complete resource Appendix. $29.95

See the Order Form next page

Order Order Form

To order books with *VISA* or MasterCard call 1-775-887-1394 Phone orders are shipped the same day received.

Yes, George, by golly, send me the following books, personally autographed and inscribed by y ou.

Name _____

Address_____City_____

State_____Zip_____

Phone number_____e mail address_____

Yes, George send me the following books, autographed and inscribed:
___Copy(ies) Hot Springs of Northern California, $12.95
___Copy(ies) Hot Springs of Nevada, $10.95
___Copy(ies) Hot Springs of the Eastern Sierra, $10.95 pap.
___Copy(ies) In the Last of the Wild West, $12.95 pap.
___Copy(ies) Rosa May: The Search For A Mining Camp Legend, $11.95
___Copy(ies) The Redlight Ladies of Virginia City, $6.95 pap.
___Copy(ies) The Guide to Bodie, $12.95 pap.
___Copy(ies) The Murders at Convict Lake, $5.95 pap.
___Copy(ies) Mark Twain: His Adventures at Aurora, $7.95 pap.
___Copy(ies) Mark Twain: His Life In Virginia City, Nevada, $10.95 pap
___Copy(ies) Mark Twain and the Jumping Frog...$8.95.
___Copy(ies) On the Road with Mark Twain $29.95 hard cover
___Copy(ies) The Songwriter's Demo Manual, $29.95 hard cover.

Shipping by postal service is $2.00 for the first book, $1 each additional book. Priority mail is $4.

Total enclosed in check or money order _____

Mail to:
Tree By The River Publishing
P.O. Box 20703-CC
Carson City, Nevada
89721